RULERS OF INDIA

Haidar Ali and Tipu Sultan

RULERS OF INDIA

Haidar Ali and Tipu Sultan

AND THE STRUGGLE WITH THE MUSALMAN POWERS OF THE SOUTH

LEWIN B. BOWRING, C.S.I.

GYAN

Published by

Gyan Publishing House
5, Ansari Road
Daryaganj, New Delhi-110002
Phone: 011-47034999, 9811692060
E-mail: books@gyanbooks.com

Distribution Network
gyanbooks.com
India, USA, Canada, UK, Australia, France

ISBN: 978-81-212-8856-9 (PB)
First Published, 1893

2nd Impression 2023

Printed at: Gyan Press, Delhi.

RULERS OF INDIA
AUTHOR: LEWIN B. BOWRING

Rulers of India

EDITED BY

SIR WILLIAM WILSON HUNTER, K.C.S.I.

C.I.E.: M.A. (OXFORD): LL.D. (CAMBRIDGE)

HAIDAR ALÍ AND TIPÚ SULTÁN

RULERS OF INDIA

Haidar Alí and Tipú Sultán

AND THE STRUGGLE WITH THE MUSALMÁN POWERS OF THE SOUTH

By LEWIN B. BOWRING, C.S.I.

FORMERLY CHIEF COMMISSIONER OF MYSORE

Oxford

AT THE CLARENDON PRESS: 1893

PREFACE

THE following sketch of the Musalmán usurpation in Mysore is an attempt to present in a popular form the career of one of the most remarkable personages who have played their parts on the stage of Indian history, together with that of his equally remarkable son—the first distinguished by the energy, enterprise, and daring which enabled him to seize a throne, and the second by his bigotry, his hostility to the English, and the fatuous obstinacy which cost him his crown and his life.

The materials for such a memoir, although often contradictory, according to the source whence they are derived, are sufficiently copious for the greater part of the narrative. The conflicting views of English, French, and native authorities regarding Haidar Alí and his son make it difficult to form an absolutely correct estimate of their career, while the limited space at his disposal precludes the writer from doing full justice to the course of events referred to in the narrative. It was a period, however, of vital importance to the future supremacy of the British in India, and an attempt has therefore been made to represent as accurately as possible the vicissitudes of the Mysore kingdom during the thirty-eight years of the usurpation by Haidar Alí and Tipú Sultán. The sketch is confined to this period, that is, from the time when Haidar Alí first brought himself prominently to notice, down to the memorable siege of Seringapatam, which ended for ever his short-lived dynasty. Although incidentally alluded to, the momentous struggle between the English and the French for supremacy in Southern India does not come within the scope of the memoir, while it has been fully dealt with in the previous volume of this Series on 'Dupleix.'

The writer would impress upon the reader that, although the narrative is mainly taken up with a long course of strife and conquests, consequent upon the disintegration of the Mughal empire, it would be unjust to impute to the people of Mysore an innate love for war, or a sanguinary disposition. On the contrary, they are an amiable race, with kindly instincts, admirable as cultivators, and possessing an ancient and valuable literature, which raised them high in the scale of civilization long before the advent of Islám. Of the professors of that faith he may also add that nowhere can be found a better type of true refinement and courtesy than the dignified and hospitable Musalmán gentleman.

L. B. B.

TORQUAY, 1893.

CONTENTS

HAIDAR ALÍ.

		PAGES
CHAP. I.	INTRODUCTORY. HAIDAR ALÍ'S ANCESTORS. THE MYSORE DYNASTY	11-16
II.	HAIDAR RISES INTO NOTICE. CONTEST FOR SUPREMACY IN SOUTHERN INDIA . . .	17-27
III.	THE PESHWÁ INVADES MYSORE	28-30
IV.	HAIDAR ASSUMES THE CONTROL OF AFFAIRS: CONQUEST OF BEDNÚR	31-39
V.	THE MARÁTHÁS INVADE MYSORE A SECOND TIME	40-41
VI.	CONQUEST OF MALABAR	42-46
VII.	THE MARÁTHÁS AGAIN ATTACK MYSORE . .	47-48
VIII.	THE NIZÁM JOINS HAIDAR ALÍ, WHO ATTACKS THE ENGLISH: WAR FROM 1767 TO 1769 .	49-58
IX.	THE MARÁTHÁS INVADE MYSORE A FOURTH TIME	59-63
X.	CONQUEST OF COORG	64-66
XI.	NEGOTIATIONS WITH RAGHUBÁ. DEATH OF MYSORE RÁJÁ. CAPTURE OF BELLARY AND GÚTTI. ATTITUDE OF THE POONA MINISTRY .	67-71
XII.	SIEGE OF CHITALDRÚG. OPERATIONS AGAINST THE MARÁTHÁS. REDUCTION OF CHITALDRÚG	72-75
XIII.	ANNEXATION OF KADAPA. HAIDAR'S DRACONIAN RULE. ROYAL MARRIAGES	76-79
XIV.	COMBINATION OF THE MARÁTHÁS AND THE NIZÁM WITH HAIDAR AGAINST THE ENGLISH. FRUITLESS NEGOTIATIONS	80-86
XV.	HAIDAR DECLARES WAR AGAINST THE ENGLISH. HIS INVASION OF MADRAS TERRITORY, AND MILITARY OPERATIONS UP TO HIS DEATH .	87-105
XVI.	HAIDAR'S CHARACTER AND ADMINISTRATION . .	106-113

TIPÚ SULTÁN.

		PAGES
CHAP. I.	TIPÚ'S ACCESSION TO THE THRONE	117–119
II.	CAPTURE OF BEDNÚR BY GENERAL MATTHEWS: ITS RECOVERY BY TIPÚ	120–123
III.	SIEGE OF MANGALORE: TIPÚ'S CRUELTIES .	124–127
IV.	COLONEL FULLARTON'S MILITARY OPERATIONS .	128–130
V.	CAMPAIGN AGAINST THE MARÁTHÁS . . .	131–134
VI.	TIPÚ'S REFORMS IN MALABAR. EMBASSIES TO EUROPE	135–138
VII.	INVASION OF TRAVANCORE	139–144
VIII.	LORD CORNWALLIS DECLARES WAR. WANT OF SUCCESS OF GENERAL MEDOWS. SIEGE OF BANGALORE. ATTACK UPON SERINGAPATAM .	145–158
IX.	MILITARY OPERATIONS OF THE MARÁTHÁS AND THE NIZÁM	159–161
X.	CAPTURE OF NANDIDRÚG. DISASTER AT COIMBATORE. STORMING OF SÁVANDRÚG. FIRST SIEGE OF SERINGAPATAM	162–173
XI.	TIPÚ'S SECRET MACHINATIONS	174–179
XII.	LORD MORNINGTON ASSUMES THE OFFICE OF GOVERNOR-GENERAL: HIS CORRESPONDENCE WITH TIPÚ	180–188
XIII.	LORD MORNINGTON DECLARES WAR AGAINST TIPÚ. FINAL SIEGE OF SERINGAPATAM. THE SULTÁN'S DEATH	189–207
XIV.	TIPÚ'S CHARACTER AND ADMINISTRATION. HIS FANATICISM AND CRUELTY	208–227
	INDEX	229–233

NOTE ON THE SPELLING OF INDIAN NAMES

The orthography of proper names follows the system adopted by the Indian Government for the *Imperial Gazetteer of India*. That system, while adhering to the popular spelling of very well-known places, such as Punjab, Poona, Deccan, Mysore, Bangalore, &c., employs in all other cases the vowels with the following uniform sounds:—

a, as in w*o*man: *á*, as in f*a*ther: *i*, as in k*i*n: *í*, as in intr*i*gue: *o*, as in cold: *u*, as in b*u*ll: *ú*, as in r*u*ral.

HAIDAR ALÍ

PEDIGREE OF THE NAWÁBS OF MYSORE.

- Muhammad Bháilól.
  - Walí Muhammad.
    - Muhammad Iliás.
      - Haidar Sáhib.
  - Alí Muhammad, or Alí Ghulám Dost Muhammad, married daughter of Sayyad Parsá Munshi.
    - Muhammad.
    - ? Muhammad Imán.
    - Fatah Muhammad, called Fatah Alí, or Shújá Sáhib, d. 1729. married Majedda Begam, daughter of Mír Akbar Alí Khán.
      - Sháhbáz Khán, or Ismáil.
        - Kádir Sáhib.
      - Walí Muhammad, died young.
      - **Haidar Alí Khán**, 1761–82. married 1. Fakhr-un-nissá, daughter of Moín-ud-dín, 2. daughter of Makdúm Sáhib.
        - **Tipú Sultán**, or Fatah Alí Khán, 1782–99.
          - Ahmad Sultán, d. 1239 H; 3 daughters.
          - Muhammad Sultán, or Ghulám Muhammad, d. 1877 A.D.; 3 sons, 3 daughters.
          - Munír-ud-dín Sultán, d. 1253 H; 1 son, 2 daughters.
          - Jamá-ud-dín Sultán, d. 1258 H; 1 son.
          - Sarwar-ud-dín Sultán, d. 1249 H; 2 daughters.
          - Shukar Ullah Sultán, d. 1233 H; 6 sons, 4 daughters.
          - Muhammad Subhán Sultán, d. 1261 H; 5 sons, 6 daughters.
          - Muhammad Yasín Sultán, d. 1849 A.D.; 8 sons, 6 daughters.
          - Moíz-ud-dín Sultán, d. 1233 H; 1 son, 3 daughters.
          - Mohí-ud-dín, or Sultán Pádsháh, d. 1226 H; 5 sons, 2 daughters.
          - Abd-ul-Khálik Sultán, d. 1222 H; 2 sons.
          - Fatah Haidar, or Haidar Alí Sultán, d. 1230 H; 7 sons, 14 daughters.
        - Karím Sháh, or Safdar Shikoh.
          - Imám Baksh; 1 son.
          - Ghulám Alí; 3 sons, 1 daughter.

HAIDAR ALÍ

CHAPTER I

INTRODUCTORY

HAIDAR ALÍ'S ANCESTORS. THE MYSORE DYNASTY.

THE terrible uprising in India in 1857, commonly called the Mutiny, has to some extent obliterated the recollection of previous events in that country; but two generations ago most people had heard of the siege of Seringapatam, while readers of the Waverley Novels were familiar with the slight story called 'The Surgeon's Daughter.' In both cases the scene lay in that part of India now known as Mysore (Maisúr), which was the cradle of one of the most daring and successful adventurers recorded in the annals of the East, and perhaps the most formidable adversary whom the British ever encountered in that region. The name of this leader of men was Haidar Alí, and although the kingdom founded by him lasted only during his own time and that of his son, Tipú Sultán—a brief space of some thirty-eight years—this short period was fruitful of events which tended to consolidate British power in India as the paramount authority.

In Hindustán, as elsewhere, when any man of vigour and energy has raised himself to a throne, it is not difficult to find for him a pedigree showing his noble descent, and it is not therefore surprising that native annalists should endeavour to prove that Haidar came from the famous race of the Korésh. According to their accounts, one of his ancestors named Hasan, who claimed Yahya as his progenitor, left Baghdád, and came to Ajmere in India, where he had a son called Walí Muhammad. This person, having quarrelled with an uncle, made his way to Gulbarga in the Deccan, and had a son named Alí Muhammad, who eventually migrated to Kolár in the eastern part of Mysore, where he died about the year 1678, having had four sons, the youngest of whom was named Fatah Muhammad[1]. Fatah Muhammad was not long in finding military employment, and by his prowess

[1] Wilks, in his history of Southern India, gives a somewhat different version of Haidar's ancestry. According to his authorities, Haidar's great-grandfather Muhammad Bháilól was a Musalmán devotee, who left the Punjab to seek his fortune in Southern India, accompanied by his sons Alí Muhammad and Walí Muhammad. He settled at Áland in the Haidarábád territory, whence the sons proceeded to Sírá in Mysore, where they found service under the Súbahdár or Governor of that place, but subsequently migrated to Kolár. Here Alí Muhammad died, and his son Fatah Muhammad, with his mother, was ejected by Walí Muhammad from the family home. The discrepancy between this account and that given in the text is not however very material. Bháilól is an Afghán name, and was that of the founder of the Lódi dynasty which was uprooted by the celebrated Mughal Bábar in 1526.

at the siege of Ganjikotá won applause, and preferment at the hands of the Súbahdár of Sírá, being raised to the rank of Náyak; but on a change of Súbahdárs, he tried to better his fortunes, first at Arcot, and then at Chittúr. Eventually he returned to Mysore, was made a Fáujdár, or military commander, and received Búdikotá as a jágír or appanage. He married first a Sayyadáni, by whom he had three sons, and subsequently two sisters (permissible by the law of Islám), whose father was a Naváyat of the race of Háshim. By the younger of these ladies he had two sons, Sháhbáz or Ismáil and Haidar [1] (the Lion), the latter of whom eventually usurped the sovereignty of Mysore.

It would occupy too much space to relate the former history of the territory now called Mysore [2], but it may be stated that at no time prior to Haidar Alí had the whole of it been governed by one ruler, or been known by this name. The ancient Hindu dynasties of Kadambas, Gangás, Chálukyas, and others, which ruled parts of it from the fifth to the twelfth centuries, had passed away, leaving no annals save those recorded on their stone-grants [3]. To them

[1] There is some uncertainty as to the year of his birth, some authorities giving 1722, and others 1717.

[2] For an account of the Mysore province, the reader is referred to *The Imperial Gazetteer of India*.

[3] Silá Sháshanas are grants on stone, generally found in the courtyards of temples, and having incised on them the descent of the donor, his feats of arms, and the nature of the benefaction, which almost always consisted of land. Támrá, or copper Shásanas, were engraved on copper-plates, through which was passed a ring,

succeeded Jáin rulers, whose memory is sustained by the beautifully carved temples at Halebid and Bélúr, while the ruins at Hampi attest the glory of the sovereigns of Vijayanagar.

In the beginning of the eighteenth century the country was occupied by petty chiefs called Pálegárs or Náyaks, who ruled various portions of it. Those of Bednúr and Chitaldrúg were the most important, but many of the smaller states were in course of time conquered and annexed by the Wodiars of Mysore proper, whose possessions on the death of Chikka Devaráj in 1704 comprised about half of the present Mysore kingdom. The history of these latter rulers, who claim a Kshatriya descent, has a certain amount of romantic interest attached to it, the first of the race who entered Mysore having been a Paladin named Vijayaráj, who at the close of the fourteenth century, with his brother Krishnaráj, left Dwárká in Káthiáwár, and proceeded to the Karnátik country. On arriving at Hadinád near Mysore, they ascertained that the daughter of the local Wodiar or prince, a man of insane mind, was about to be forcibly married to a neighbouring chief who, in case of refusal, threatened to seize her father's possessions. The brothers by stratagem slew the obnoxious suitor and annexed his territory, while Vijayaráj himself wedded the distressed damsel, adopting at the same time

stamped with the seal of the donor, each dynasty having its own emblem, in one case an elephant, in others a boar, or a hanumán monkey.

the tenets of the Lingáyat faith[1]. Such was the commencement of the rule of the present Mysore sovereigns, who, though of noble descent, were, unlike most of their predecessors in the Karnátik, of foreign origin.

For a period of two hundred years they held the status of petty chieftains only, but in 1609 Ráj Wodiar, seventh in descent from Vijayaráj, taking advantage of the weakness of the decaying Vijayanagar kingdom, to which Mysore was nominally subject, seized the fortress of Srírangapatan (Seringapatam), and made it the seat of his government. Shortly afterwards he renounced the Língáyat faith, reverting to the worship of Vishnu, as practised by his ancestors. From this time he and his successors gradually extended their territory by conquest till, on the death of Chikka Devaráj, their possessions yielded a considerable revenue. In order to conciliate the Emperor Aurangzeb, who was said to contemplate the invasion of the Mysore country, Chikka Devaráj despatched an embassy in 1699 which was favourably received by the Great Mughal, who bestowed upon the Rájá, as he was now styled, the title of Jaga Deva, and an ivory throne, which was afterwards used on the installation of his successors. Chikka Devaráj was a brave soldier and an excellent administrator, but those who followed him being incompetent rulers, all power, as in the case of the descendants of the famous Sivají,

[1] The Lingáyats are worshippers of Siva, and wear the *phallus* in a small silver box, which is suspended by a string from the neck.

fell virtually into the hands of the minister, the Rájás being mere puppets, who were put on the throne or deposed at the caprice of the leading men of the State. The direct descent ended in 1733 with the demise of Dodda Krishnaráj (or Krishnaráj the Elder), after which time new chiefs were elected at the pleasure of the Dalwái, or Commander-in-Chief, who usurped all the functions of government.

PEDIGREE OF THE MYSORE RÁJÁS.

Vijayaráj, 1399.

Ráj Wodiar, 1577-1616.

Chikka Devaráj, or Devaráj the younger, 1671-1704/5.

Kánthi Rái, 1704/5-16. The dumb Rájá.

Dodda Krishnaráj, or Krishnaráj the elder, 1716-33[1].

Chámráj, adopted, 1733-36, died in prison.

Chikka Krishnaráj, or Krishnaráj the younger, adopted, 1736-66.

Nanjráj, 1766-71, strangled.	Chámráj, 1771-76.	Chámráj of Kárúhalli, 1776-96, adopted, chosen by Haidar Alí.
		Mummadi Krishnaráj, or Krishnaráj the Third, 1799-1868.

[1] The dates given for the accession of this chief and his successor vary slightly from the generally-received record, but as the report from which they are taken gives the *name* of the Hindu cycle year, they are presumably correct.

CHAPTER II

HAIDAR RISES INTO NOTICE—CONTEST FOR SUPREMACY IN SOUTHERN INDIA

DURING the reign of the Emperor Sháhjahán, when his son Aurangzeb was Viceroy of the Deccan, a great part of the Karnátik was overrun by the troops of the King of Bíjapur under the command of Ran Dulhá Khán and Sháhjí, father of the great Sivají. But when Aurangzeb mounted the throne, he determined to crush both the Maráthás and the Musalmán sovereign of Bíjapur, which capital was taken in 1687, when Sírá became the headquarters of an imperial deputy. This post, at the time when Fatah Muhammad, Haidar's father, distinguished himself, as previously mentioned, was held by Dargáh Kuli Khán, who was nominated to it in 1729. He was succeeded by his son Abd-ur-Rasúl Khán, in whose service Fatah Muhammad was killed, with his chief, while fighting against Saádat Ullah Khán, the Nawáb of Arcot. His children, with their mother, were tortured and plundered by the son of the late Súbahdár, and sent adrift to seek a refuge elsewhere.

They proceeded to Bangalore. When the elder son Sháhbáz was old enough, he obtained a small post as a subordinate officer, but soon rose to the command of 200 horse and 1,000 foot, forming part of a force which was despatched in 1749 by the Mysore Dalwái to besiege Devanhalli[1], twenty-three miles north of Bangalore. He was here joined by his brother Haidar, who, though serving only as a volunteer, attracted attention by his gallantry and daring. He is described as being at this time of irregular habits, and addicted to low pursuits, but he was a keen sportsman and full of dash and energy. He was wholly illiterate, and indeed never learned to write. This, however, was common enough in those days, when most chiefs were content with affixing to papers either their seal or some fanciful device in lieu of a signature[2].

The Mysore minister at that time was Nanjráj, who, pleased with Haidar's courage, gave him the command of a small body of troops, and shortly afterwards, when a force was despatched to Arcot, in accordance with instructions from the Nizám Násir Jang, Haidar and his brother accompanied the army.

It may be appropriate to our narrative to give here some account of the principal chiefs with whose history

[1] Halli in Kannadí or Kanarese has the same meaning as Palli in Tamil, signifying a town or village, as in the word Trichinápalli, commonly called Trichinopoli. The word 'úr,' so often found in the names of places in Southern India, has the same signification.

[2] Many of the minor chiefs in Orissa still make use of this form of attestation, one drawing a peacock, another a tiger's head, a third a conch-shell, a fourth a flower as his sign-manual, and so forth.

the fortune of Haidar and his son was closely interwoven. On the death of Aurangzeb in 1707, the supremacy of the Great Mughals virtually terminated, as, owing to the incompetence of his successors, enemies rose up on every side, while the Imperial deputies in Southern India either made themselves independent, or succumbed to the superior force of Maráthás and Patháns. Foremost among those who set aside the royal authority was the Nizám, who claimed descent from Abú Bakr, while among his remote ancestors were Muhammad Bahá-ud-dín Baghdádi, who founded the order of the Nakshbandi Darveshes, and Shekh Shaháb-ud-dín Sohrwádi, a celebrated Súfi or mystic. The family settled, it is stated, at Samána[1], now in the State of Patiála in the Punjab, and one of its members, Ábid Khán, was killed at Golconda while fighting in the ranks of the Imperial army. His son, Ghází or Shaháb-ud-dín, was appointed governor of Gujarát, and the latter's son, Kamar-ud-dín, Cháin Kalij Khán, was in 1713 nominated Nizám-ul-mulk, or Viceroy of the Deccan, with a nominal control over all tho royal possessions in Southern India. The pedigree on the next page shows the descent.

[1] The only authority for this is a statement made to the writer when encamped at the place.

PEDIGREE OF THE NIZÁMS.

Khwájah Ábid Kalij Khán, Governor of Ajmere.

Mír Shaháb-ud-dín, or Ghází-ud-dín Khán, Governor of Gujarát.

Mír Kamar-ud-dín, first Nizám, 1713–48.

- Mír Ghází-ud-dín, ancestor of the Báoni Nawáb.
- Mír Muhammad Násir Jang, second Nizám, 1748-50.
- Mír Asaf-ud-dáulah, Salábat Jang, fourth Nizám, 1751–61.
- Mír Shújá-ul-mulk, Basálat Jang.
- Mír Nizám Alí Khán, fifth Nizám, 1761–1803.
  - Mír Ahmad Khán, Alí Jáh.
  - Mír Akbar Alí Khán, Sikandar Jáh, sixth Nizám, 1803–28.
  - Mír Subhán Alí Khán, Farídún Jáh, and five other sons.
- Mír Násir-ul-mulk, Mughal Alí Khán.
- daughter.
  - Hidáyat Mohí-ud-dín, Muzaffar Jang, third Nizám, 1750–51.

The chief next in importance was the Nawáb of Arkát (Arcot). After Aurangzeb had subjugated the Bíjapur and Golconda kingdoms, he sent a force under Zulfikár Khán, with one Dáúd Khán as second in command, to reduce the fortress of Jinjí or Chenji[1], then held by Ráma, son of Sivají. The place was carried by assault in 1698, but as it proved unhealthy, Arcot was in 1716 selected as the capital. The imperial deputy, Kásim Khán, having been assassinated, Zulfikár Khán was nominated as his successor, and after him Dáúd Khán; but this chief, being summoned to Delhi to aid the party which ultimately put Sháh Álam on the throne, left Muhammad Saíd, called Saádat Ullah Khán, as his substitute. Saádat Ullah Khán ruled with success from 1710 to 1732, but, having no son, left the *masnad* to his nephew Dost Alí Khán, who invaded Mysore, but was disgracefully defeated by the troops of Rájá Chikka Krishnaráj. It was during the rule of this Nawáb that his son-in-law, Hussén Dost Khán, better known as Chandá Sáhib, acquired by fraud the territory of Trichinopoli, and subsequently sided with the

[1] This remarkable fortress is in South Arcot, and is built on three hills, from 500 to 600 feet high, connected together by strong walls of circumvallation. The Rájágiri, or principal hill, is inaccessible on all sides, save the south-west, where a steep ravine permits access to the top; but even here three lines of walls protected the citadel from an assault, the only approach to the summit being by a bridge thrown over a chasm, opposite to which was a gateway, with flanking defences. The place was first fortified by the Vijayanagar kings in the fourteenth century, and after falling into many hands, was captured by the French in 1750 in a brilliant manner.

French against the English. Safdar Alí succeeded as Nawáb, but was assassinated in 1742. His infant son Muhammad Saíd was installed by the Nizám, but was murdered within a year, when Anwar-ud-dín, his guardian, was confirmed as Nawáb by the Nizám. The succession of the several Nawábs of Arcot is as follows:—

Muhammad Saíd, or Saádat Ullah Khan, 1710–32.

Dost Alí Khán, his nephew, 1732–40.

- Safdar Alí Khán, 1740–42, assassinated.
  - Muhammad Saíd Khán, 1742–43.
- daughter, married Hussén Dost Khán, or Chandá Sáhib.

Anwar-ud-dín, 1743–49.

- Máhfúz Khán.
- Wáláját Muhammad Alí, 1749–95.
  - Umdat-ul-Umrá, 1795–1801.

There were three other prominent Musalmán chiefs, namely the Pathán Nawábs of Kadapa, Karnúl, and Shánúr or Sávanúr[1], while Morári Ráo Ghorpara[2], a Maráthá, ruled at Gútti; all of these being, nominally at least, subordinate to the Nizám. These somewhat dry details are necessary to elucidate the course of subsequent events.

[1] The first two of these Houses are extinct, but the Sávanúr Nawáb still holds an estate in the Dhárwár district of the Bombay Presidency, comprising twenty-five villages with a rental of £5,660.

[2] This chief's descendant is the Rájá of Sandúr in the Bellary district of Madras, his territory having an area of 140 square miles, with an income of £4,500. The sanitarium of Rámandrúg is in Sandúr.

The occasion which, in 1749, led to the despatch of the troops from Mysore, with whom Haidar was serving, was a contest for the Nizámat between Násir Jang and his nephew Muzaffar Jang, the latter of whom had been nominated as his successor by Kamar-ud-dín, who died in 1748; but Násir Jang, being on the spot, seized the throne, calling to his aid the chiefs just mentioned, as well as the Rájá of Mysore, who was tributary to the Nizám. Muhammad Alí of Arcot joined his standard, as also a contingent of British troops under Major Lawrence. On the other side were marshalled the forces of Muzaffar Jang, aided by Chandá Sáhib, and a body of French troops under Colonel De Bussy. It is foreign to the purpose of this memoir to relate the long struggle for supremacy between the two European powers which took place at this period, and the reader is referred to Colonel Malleson's excellent work on *The History of the French in India*, in which ample details will be found on the subject. It may suffice to say that had the masterly diplomacy and genius of the great Dupleix been adequately supported by the French Government, the nation which he represented might probably have dominated the whole of Southern India. But the magnificent scheme which he originated for founding an Eastern empire, and in which he was ably seconded by De Bussy, was frustrated by the jealousy of his compatriots and the indifference of his Government. Dupleix himself, having been recalled to France in 1754, died there in abject poverty and broken-hearted a few years afterwards.

Probably neither the English nor the French authorities cared much about the alleged rights of either of the claimants of the Nizámat, but were bent only on supporting the one who would be likely to advance their own interests. In any case, the contested sovereignty was an authority usurped from the Great Mughal, while the Arcot Nawáb was really only a deputy, removable at pleasure by the Nizám. Dupleix favoured Chandá Sáhib. This chief was under obligations to him for hospitality shown to his family at Pondicherry and for his release from imprisonment by the Maráthás, but Dupleix' support of Chandá Sáhib and his advocacy of the pretensions of Muzaffar Jang were prompted only by his astute policy, which sought any available counterpoise to British influence. On the other hand, the English at Madras allied themselves with Násir Jang and his representative Muhammad Alí (whose father Anwar-ud-dín had been killed at Ambúr fighting against the French), for precisely similar reasons, that is, to foil Dupleix in his designs.

In the first encounter which ensued between the opposing forces, Násir Jang was victorious (partly owing to a mutiny among the French troops), Muzaffar Jang being taken prisoner, while Chandá Sáhib fled to Pondicherry. Násir Jang then retired to Arcot[1],

[1] The citadel in Arcot, which was so brilliantly defended by Clive in 1751, was in a rectangular fortress surrounded by a shallow

but Dupleix having shortly afterwards seized, through De Bussy's daring, the strong fortress of Jinji, and won over to his side the Pathán Nawábs, Násir Jang was compelled again to take the field. In the short campaign which followed Násir was treacherously killed by the Kadapa Nawáb, while Muzaffar Jang was installed as Nizám by the French, and Muhammad Alí fled precipitately to Trichinopoli. The Mysore troops on this occasion bore themselves bravely. Haidar, with the mercenary instinct of a freebooter, took advantage of the confusion to seize, with the aid of his Bedar followers, a large amount of the late Nizám's treasure, with which he retreated to Mysore. Before doing so, he paid a visit to Pondicherry[1], where he formed a high opinion of the discipline of the French troops and of the skill of their engineer officers.

In 1751 we find Haidar again on active service, accompanying, as commandant of the cavalry, a Mysore force which was despatched by the Dalwái to co-operate with Muhammad Alí, who promised to cede to Mysore Trichinopoli and all the country south of it to the *ghâts* on the eastward. It is not proposed to discuss the incidents of the long war which now

ditch, but is now in ruins; as is also the greater part of the 'Shahar Panáh,' a rampart five miles in circumference, 24 feet broad at the base, and 12 feet at the top.

[1] Pondicherry, called by the natives Pudûchéri, was founded by F. Martin in 1674. It comprises three divisions, viz. Pondicherry, Villiánûr, and Báhûr, containing 93 villages with 141 hamlets, and has an area of 112 square miles.

took place, and was not terminated till the end of 1754, when a treaty, much to the disadvantage of the French, was concluded. The Mysore commander, Nanjráj, played a double part, intriguing both with the English and the French, but eventually siding with the latter. Foiled in his attempts to obtain possession of Trichinopoli, owing to the treachery of Muhammad Alí, he was at last compelled to return to Mysore in 1755, having spent large sums of money unprofitably.

During the course of the military operations in this campaign Haidar seized several guns belonging to an English convoy which was cut off in the Pudukottai territory between Tanjore and Trichinopoli, and largely increased his force of Bedars. His nominal command now aggregated 1,500 horse and 3,000 infantry, besides less disciplined troops. To assist him in organizing the system of plundering, which he carried on for many years, he took into his service a Maráthá Bráhman, named Khande Ráo, whose literary qualifications made amends for his own want of education. But although compelled to have recourse to this extraneous aid, Haidar had a most retentive memory, which, added to his acute penetration, made it very difficult to deceive him.

In the same year that witnessed the withdrawal of the Mysore troops from their abortive expedition, that is in 1755, Haidar was appointed Fáujdár or military governor of Dindigal, now in the Madura district of Madras, a stronghold which the Mysore State had acquired ten years previously. Here he established an arsenal under the superintendence of French artificers whose services he obtained from Pondicherry. He also augmented the numbers of his troops, and accumulated considerable wealth by plundering the chiefs in the neighbourhood. The position which Haidar thus attained was the foundation of his future influence, although it was not till the acquisition of Bednúr, as will be hereafter related, that he actually usurped the supreme control.

CHAPTER III

THE PESHWÁ INVADES MYSORE

WHILE the Mysore army under Nanjráj was still engaged in the hostilities above narrated, the new Nizám, Salábat Jang[1], accompanied by M. de Bussy, whose exploits in the Deccan had made him famous, marched on Seringapatam, and demanded a large sum as arrears of tribute, only a third of which, or eighteen lacs, could be raised on the spot. Even this sum was collected with great difficulty, the minister Devaráj resorting to every expedient to avoid payment. But, alarmed on hearing that the Maráthás were preparing also to invade Mysore, he resorted to forcible measures, such as plundering the temples and handing over the Crown jewels, to satisfy the Nizám's demands. The rumour that the Maráthás were approaching proved to be true. In March, 1757, the Peshwá[2] Bálájí Bájí Ráo suddenly appeared before the capital, exacting the payment of a heavy contri-

[1] His nephew Muzaffar Jang was deposed in 1751 by a conspiracy, headed by the Nawábs of Karnúl and Sávanúr, when Salábat Jang was, owing to the influence of M. de Bussy, put on the throne.

[2] The Peshwás still professed to be merely the ministers of the Satára Rájás, having on their seals a fictitious device testifying to

bution, of which five lacs of rupees were paid in cash, while certain districts were surrendered in pledge for an additional sum of twenty-seven lacs.

Haidar Alí, who had been summoned to Mysore, owing to disputes between Devaráj and his brother Nanjráj, found the troops in a state of mutiny owing to arrears of pay. By his address, and a careful scrutiny of the accounts, he was enabled to pay all legitimate claims, and to disband more than 4,000 men, while he seized the ringleaders of the revolt and plundered them. After the Maráthá troops had withdrawn into their own territory, Haidar counselled evading the payment due to Poona from the assigned districts, but the Peshwá, resenting this breach of the obligations entered into by Mysore, despatched in 1759 a force under Gopál Hari to annex this domain. Having accomplished this task, the Maráthá leader invested Bangalore, and seized Chennapatam, between that place and Seringapatam. But Haidar, who had been placed in command of the Mysore army, deputed a favourite officer named Lutf Alí Bég to surprise Chennapatam, a feat which he successfully accomplished, thus compelling Gopál Hari to relinquish the blockade of Bangalore. For some months the rival forces confronted one another, but at length the

their nominal subservience, although they were the 'de facto' rulers. For instance, Bálájí's seal bore the following inscription :—

Srí Rájá Sáhú Narapati		Rájá Sáhú, King of men,
Harsha Nidhán	i.e.	Treasury of delight ;
Báláji Báji Ráo		Báláji Báji Ráo,
Mukhya Pradhán.		Chief Minister.

Maráthá chief, foiled by the incessant activity and energy of his adversary, agreed to withdraw his troops, and to relinquish the pledged districts, on condition that thirty-two lacs should be paid by Mysore. Half of this sum was speedily raised by a forced contribution, while the Maráthá bankers accepted Haidar's personal security for the remainder, the realization of the revenues of the pledged territory meanwhile being confided to him. On the departure of the Maráthás, Haidar returned to Seringapatam, and received from the grateful Rájá the title of Fatah Haidar Bahádur, in recognition of his services on this occasion. This style he invariably used afterwards on all grants made by him. Previously he had been known simply as Haidar Náyak.

FAMILY TREE OF THE PESHWÁS.

- (1) Bálájí Viswanáth of Srivardhan in Chául, 1714–20.
  - (2) Bájí Ráo Balál, 1720–40.
    - (3) Bálájí Bájí Ráo, 1740–61.
      - Viswás Ráo, killed in 1761 at Pánipat.
      - (4) Madhu Ráo, 1761–72, s. p.
      - (5) Náráyan Ráo, 1772–73, murdered.
        - (7) Madhu Ráo Náráyan, 1782–95.
    - (6) Raghunáth Ráo, or Raghubá, 1773–82.
      - (8) Bájí Ráo Raghunáth, 1795–1818, deposed.
        - Dhúndhú Panth. Náná Sáhib (adopted), rebelled 1857
  - Chimnáji.

CHAPTER IV

Haidar assumes the control of affairs—Conquest of Bednúr

The young Rájá Chikka Krishnaráj of Mysore had long smarted under the thraldom of his Mayor of the Palace, Nanjráj, and it occurred to the dowager queen that advantage might be taken of the ascendancy over the troops which Haidar had acquired to get rid of the obnoxious minister. This was successfully achieved with the aid of Khande Ráo, but the effect was to exchange King Log for King Stork, for Haidar, having practically command of the army and of the revenue of nearly half the kingdom, kept the Rájá in the same state of dependence as before. Khande Ráo was then won over by the Ráni, and by his advice recourse was had to the Maráthás, at a time when the greater part of Haidar's troops were engaged in operations below the *ghâts*, and a force was despatched to Seringapatam to attack him. Taken by surprise, Haidar was compelled to flee in haste, leaving his family behind him, and, attended by only a few faithful followers, reached Bangalore, having ridden ninety-eight miles in twenty hours.

This was a critical period in Haidar's career.

Having lost all his treasure and his artillery, his sole hope was in the troops under the command of his brother-in-law, Makdúm Alí, then engaged in warfare in the Arcot district, while the main object of the treacherous Khande Ráo, who owed everything to Haidar's patronage, was to annihilate this force with the aid of the Maráthás. Fortune however favoured Haidar. For just at this time the Peshwá's army was signally defeated in the memorable battle fought against Ahmad Sháh Abdáli at Pánípat in 1761, and the Maráthá force in Mysore, commanded by Visají Pandit, was recalled hastily to Poona, the only conditions exacted being the cession of the Báramaháls[1] and the payment of three lacs of rupees. The money was paid, but the territory mentioned was never surrendered, while Haidar, relieved from the pressure which had been put upon him, proceeded to encounter Khande Ráo at Nanjangúd, twenty-seven miles south of Seringapatam. He was, however, defeated. Haidar then adopted the singular course of throwing himself as a suppliant at the feet of Nanjráj, the late Minister, who, completely deceived by his professions of fidelity, was weak enough to put him in command of a respectable body of troops, and to give him the title of

[1] The districts referred to are in the northern part of the Salem district of Madras, the hills which enclose the greater part of them protruding from the plateau of Mysore, the passes into which they practically commanded. The territory nominally comprised twelve districts, whence the name of 'Báramahál,' but the precise extent of the territory so called seems to have varied at different times. The excellent *Salem District Manual* derives the word Mahal from the Persian for a palace, but it is more probably Mahál, i.e. a district.

Dalwái, or commander-in-chief. Armed with this authority Haidar endeavoured to effect a junction with the force at Seringapatam, but was outmanœuvred by Khande Ráo, and his ruin seemed inevitable. But he fabricated letters in the name of Nanjráj to the officers of the latter's troops, desiring them to surrender Khande Ráo in accordance with a pre-arranged agreement. These letters were designedly carried to Khande Ráo, who, fearing a conspiracy, abandoned his army, and fled to Seringapatam.

Haidar, hearing of Khande Ráo's flight, attacked his troops, and gained an easy victory, capturing all his guns and baggage, while the infantry readily sided with the conqueror. For some months he was actively engaged in reducing all the forts below the passes which had come into possession of Khande Ráo. During these operations he added largely to his following, and when his preparations were complete, he assembled his army on the banks of the Káveri, opposite to Seringapatam. After a few days of apparent inactivity, Haidar suddenly dashed across the river, and surprised the enemy's camp, scattering dismay among the troops, who at once acknowledged his authority. He then, after arranging for the Rájá's personal expenditure, demanded that the control of affairs should be made over to him, and that his treacherous friend Khande Ráo should be surrendered to his mercy. A story is told as to this last incident, to the effect that the ladies of the palace interceded for the unfortunate Bráhman, whereupon Haidar replied that he would cherish him like a *tótá* (parrot), a promise which he kept by keeping him in an iron cage, and feeding him on rice and milk till the end of his life.

The Nizám Salábat Jang, who was of inferior capacity, had two younger brothers, named Basálat Jang and Nizám Alí Khán, by the latter of whom he was deposed and imprisoned in 1761. The other brother, Basálat Jang, who was in charge of the Adoni district bordering on Mysore, deemed the occasion favourable for extending his own possessions, and accordingly meditated the reduction of Sírá; but finding the place strongly occupied by the Maráthás, who had seized it four years before, he advanced upon Hoskote, not far from Bangalore. Haidar, ascertaining that he was unable to seize that town, entered into negotiations with him, with the result that Haidar, on the payment of three lacs, was appointed Nawáb of Sírá, and proclaimed as Haidar Alí Khán Bahádur, a title which Basálat Jang had no authority whatever to bestow, but which was afterwards openly assumed by Haidar.

On the departure of Basálat Jang, after the occupation of Sírá, Haidar Alí turned his attention to the reduction of the Pálegárs of Chikka Ballapúr, Raidrúg, Harpanhalli, and Chitaldrúg, all of whom were compelled to submit to his authority and to pay tribute. While Haidar was encamped near Chitaldrúg, his assistance was solicited to replace on the *masnad* an individual who gave himself out to be the legitimate Rájá of Bednúr, a chiefdom in the Malnád, a hill country to the westward, and better known as the territory of the Náyaks of Kiladi. Kiladi, now a petty village in the north-west of Mysore, was the homestead of two brothers who, about the year 1560, having found a treasure, and duly sacrificed a human victim, according to the barbarous practice of the time, received from the Rájá of Vijayanagar a grant for the territory which their wealth enabled them to overrun. Their descendants moved the capital to Ikkeri[1], ten miles to the south, where Venkatappa Náyak was ruling at the time when the Italian traveller Pietro della Valle visited this part of India about 1623. Della Valle, who had great powers of observation, gives an interesting account of the social and religious customs of the Lingáyats, to which sect the chief belonged. Della Valle was in the suite of the Portuguese envoy, for whose amusement various entertainments were provided, among which Della Valle mentions the Kolahátá dance, in which the girls held short sticks in their hands, which they struck against one another as they danced, singing as they circled round in the piazza of the temple. This dance is still practised by the Coorgs[2].

[1] In the temple at Ikkeri are curious effigies of some of the Náyaks, one of whom, who was mad, is represented as fettered hand and foot. The distance between the pillars of this building was adopted as the standard for measuring the space between the several trees of a betel-nut plantation.

[2] Della Valle appears to have married a Syrian lady, who died

In the distracted times when the Vijayanagar dynasty was tottering towards its fall, Ikkeri was considered unsafe as a capital, so the chief's head-quarters were moved in 1640 by Sivappa Náyak to Bednúr, or Bidurúrú, i.e. the town of bamboos. This was a central position in a difficult hilly country, surrounded by thick forests, whilst the Náyak fortified the town with strong outposts extending several miles, which made it, if not impregnable, at any rate sufficiently strong to defy all attacks by undisciplined troops. Horses were rarely found in the country, while no forage could be procured for them without great difficulty. The rough tracks were traversed by pack-bullocks, which, at the risk of fractured limbs, descended the rugged passes leading to the coast, laden with rice and betel-nut, and bringing back cloths and salt, while in every pass and gorge was a guard of soldiers, who not only stopped all hostile invaders, but acted as custom-house officers, and levied toll on all imports and exports.

Sivappa Náyak was an able administrator, who took practical steps to test the real value of land by

during his absence from his native land. He carried her remains however to Rome, and deposited them in the family vault in the church of Ara Coeli, erecting a large cross, on the foot of which was inscribed the following epitaph in 1626 :—

Maani Gieroidae, Heroinae
Praestantissimae
Petri De Valle Perini uxoris
Mortales exuviae.

See Notes in Goethe's 'West-Oestlicher Divan' on Pietro della Valle.

cultivating various crops and noting the produce and the market-rates, by which he arrived at a fair notion of the capabilities of each description of soil, and was enabled to fix an equitable assessment. During his rule the town increased rapidly, and became eventually of such importance as to merit the appellation of *nagar*, or city, the name which it still bears, while the possessions of the chief included not only the greater part of the Malnád, or hill region, but also the plain country below the passes extending to the western coast, now called Kánara. In fact the territory comprised nearly 10,000 square miles, while the Náyaks were at the beginning of the eighteenth century of greater importance than the Rájás of Mysore.

In this secluded region the Náyaks held undisputed sway for two hundred years, but did not advance their frontiers to any extent after the death of Sivappa Náyak, whose successors merely retained the possessions he had won. In 1755 Baswappa Náyak, the ruling chief, died, leaving his widow Vírammají as guardian of an adopted son named Chenna Baswaia. This youth is said to have been murdered by the widow and her paramour, but the claimant who was presented to Haidar averred that he was in effect the heir alleged to have been killed, and that he had escaped the machinations of the Ráni and her lover.

Haidar, who derided the idea of hereditary rights, and was as unscrupulous as he was avaricious, was not slow to avail himself of the opportunity of attacking Bednúr on pretence of restoring the fugitive to his lawful position. In the beginning of 1763 he set out on this expedition, distributing his troops into four columns, and having seized Shimoga, where he found four lacs of rupees, proceeded on to Kúmsi. Here he found the imprisoned minister of the late Rájá, who readily undertook to be his guide through the wild country between Kúmsi and the capital. The affrightened Ráni, hearing of his advance, twice offered him large sums of money, but Haidar pressed onwards, rejecting all overtures, and the Ráni fled to the fortress of Balálráidrúg[1]. Acting on the information imparted by the ex-minister, Haidar, after ordering a false attack, passed through the outworks by a secret path, and suddenly made his appearance in the city. In an instant all was confusion, the inhabitants fleeing to the woods, while the Ráni's guards, struck with fear, offered no resistance, but contented themselves with firing the palace. Haidar however promptly extinguished the flames, and knowing well the reputed wealth of the town, set to work at once to appropriate the booty by systematically sealing up all the principal houses, the palace, and public offices.

The value of the property thus acquired was reputed at twelve millions sterling, and Haidar attributed to this conquest his future successes. He made short

[1] This fortress is forty miles south of Bednúr. Some accounts state that she fled to Káulidrúg, another fort, only ten miles distant, which was taken after a month's siege.

work of the Ráni and her lover, who were arrested at Balálráidrúg, and, together with her adopted son Sómasekhara and the pretended claimant, forwarded to Madgiri, a hill fort in the eastern part of Mysore.

Haidar at first thought of making Bednúr, which he now called Haidarnagar, his capital, and formed designs for building there a palace and arsenal, with a local mint, besides constructing a dockyard on the coast. But a severe attack of illness, and a conspiracy in which many hundred persons were implicated, seem to have deterred him from this project. Three hundred of the conspirators were hanged, and all signs of revolt suppressed. His acute judgment soon showed him that by confining himself to the hill country he would lose his preponderating influence in Mysore proper.

CHAPTER V

The Maráthás invade Mysore a second time

Haidar was conscious also that, by having ousted the Maráthás from the Sírá district, when he obtained the sham title of Nawáb from Basálat Jang, he had incurred the resentment of the Peshwá, as well as that of the ruling Nizám. He therefore, after conquering the small territory of Sunda, north of Bednúr, availed himself of the aid of Razá Alí Khán, son of Chandá Sáhib, who had served with the French, to train and discipline his troops, preparing himself for the inevitable struggle before him. Madhu Ráo, who had succeeded his father, Báláji Bájí Ráo, as Peshwá in 1761, was an able and energetic ruler, and ill disposed to submit tamely to the insult put upon him by Haidar. He made extensive preparations to compel the latter to surrender the territory he had usurped. Haidar, on his part, knowing what a formidable enemy he had to meet, endeavoured to win over to his side the Nawáb of Sávanúr[1], but failing in his attempts,

[1] The Mysore annalist, Mír Hussón Alí Khán, states that this Nawáb had rendered assistance to the Ráni of Bednúr, when that place was captured by Haidar, who in consequence determined to punish him; but this writer's account is so confused, and the dates given by him are so clearly wrong, that little reliance can be placed upon his narrative.

attacked that chief and ravaged his country, seizing also the fortress of Dhárwár on the other side of the Tungábhadra. In order to check his advance, the Peshwá pushed on Gopál Ráo, the chief of Míraj, with a considerable force to attack Haidar, but the latter, notwithstanding his inferiority in numbers, obtained a victory. Soon, however, the main body of the Maráthá aımy advanced to meet him, and a bloody contest ensued near Rattihalli, south of Sávanúr, in which, in spite of his skilful manœuvres, Haidar was overwhelmed by the Maráthá horse, and signally defeated, losing the best portion of his troops.

To such a stress was Haidar now reduced that he had to flee with a few cavalry to the woods of the Bednúr country, and although Madhu Ráo's advance was for a time checked by the rainy season, he soon crossed the Tungábhadra, and pursued so vigorously that Haidar, hemmed in on all sides by the Maráthás, was forced to despatch his family and treasure to Seringapatam, and to sue for peace. Madhu Ráo consented, on condition that all the territory formerly held by Morári Ráo of Gútti should be restored, that Sávanúr should be surrendered, and that thirty-two lacs of rupees should be paid as an indemnity for the expenses incurred by the Maráthás. Haidar was not however disturbed in the possession of Sírá, or of the tracts wrested by him from the neighbouring Pálegárs.

CHAPTER VI

Conquest of Malabar

It is a remarkable fact that, although his fortunes seemed now to be reduced to the lowest ebb, Haidar immediately set about planning fresh conquests in another direction. As soon as order was restored in the eastern part of Mysore, where, owing to his defeat by the Maráthás, an insurrection had broken out, he turned his eyes to an invasion of Malabar on the west coast, on the plea that it formed part of the Bednúr principality. This region was first made known to Europeans by the voyage of Vasco da Gama, whose exploits are recorded in the celebrated *Lusiad* of Camoens. The seventh and eighth cantos of that poem give an interesting account of the interviews between the Portuguese hero and the Samúri or Zamorin[1].

[1] 'Da terra os naturaes lhe chamam *Gate*,
Do pô do qual pequena quantidade
Se estende hûa fralda estreita, que combate
Do mar a natural ferocidade:
Aqui de outras cidades, sem debate,
Calecut tem a illustre dignidade

The region was originally called Kerala. It had been held by a chief styled Perumál Chéramán, a deputy of the kings of the Chéra dynasty, whose dominion appears to have extended over all the country west of the *ghâts*, from Gokarnam in North Kánara down to about the ninth degree of north latitude. Tradition says that the last of these Viceroys became a Musalmán about the year 825 A.D., and resolved to go to Mecca, but, before doing so, he divided his possessions among his principal chiefs. To the Chirakkal or Kolattiri chief he left his regalia and the northern part of his territory; to the Utayavar of Venát, ancestor of the Travancore Rájá, the southern part; to the Perimpatappa chief, who is supposed to have been his son, Cochin; and to the Zamorin his sword, and as much country as the crowing of a cock could be heard over[1]. The language spoken in this part of Southern India is Malayálim, a Dravidian tongue

De cabeça de Imperio, rica, e bella :
Samorí se intitula o Senhor della.'

Verse xxii.

'Esta Provincia, cujo porto agora
Tomado tendes, Malabar se chama :
Do culto antigo os idolos adora,
Que cá por estas partes se derrama :
De diversos Reis he, mas d' hum só fora
N' outro tempo, segundo a antigua fama :
Saramâ Perimal foi derradeiro
Rei, que este Reino teve unido, e inteiro.'

Verse xxxii. Canto vii.

[1] Another version is that the partition referred to was made on his death-bed, but although the cause assigned for the bequests varies as represented respectively by Hindu or Musalmán authorities, the fact of the division is universally accepted.

closely allied to Tamil; and from time immemorial the matriarchal system prevailed, that is, on the death of a chief, for instance, his sister's sons succeeded, to the exclusion of his own sons, while females were adopted in case of failure of direct issue. It was formerly, and is perhaps to some extent still, the custom among the Náirs, who form the bulk of the population, that one woman should marry several brothers[1]. At an early period, owing to the constant commercial relations with Arabia, Islám was introduced among the Náirs, and the descendants of the mixed race, half-Arab and half-Hindu, were called Mápillas[2]—a hardy military race, but bigoted and fanatical.

Haidar entered the country on the invitation of Alí Rájá of Cannanore, a feudatory of the Kolattiri chief, who aimed at independence. He also claimed from the Zamorin a large sum due to Mysore, which that chief had engaged to pay in order to buy off Haidar's troops when, in 1757, they had espoused the cause of his rival, the Pálghát Rájá. Owing to the gallant resistance of the Náirs, and to the difficulty of forcing

[1] When one of the brothers visited the wife, he left his sandals and his weapons in charge of a servant in the porch, as a sign that the lady was engaged. The wife had the care of the children, who would refer to the husbands of the mother, but never to the father, whom indeed it would be difficult to identify. The custom is of great antiquity, and is illustrated by the story of the celebrated Pándavas and their common spouse Dráupadi.

[2] Said to be a contraction of Mahá (great) and piḷḷa (child). Some derive the word from Má (mother) and piḷḷa, and others again from Mocha and piḷḷa, because the fathers came originally from Arabia.

his way through the thick forests which impeded his progress, Haidar's losses were heavy. But after determined opposition on the part of the enemy, and tremendous carnage in their ranks, he succeeded in reaching Kalikat (Calicut), when the Zamorin tendered his submission. Haidar received him kindly, and settled his military contribution at four lacs of sequins, but, suspecting treachery, sent troops to occupy Calicut; and as the Zamorin delayed payment, he and his minister were imprisoned, the latter being tortured. The Zamorin, fearing a similar disgrace, set fire to the house in which he was confined, and perished in the flames. The chiefs of Cochin and Pálghát at once bowed their heads to the conqueror, and Haidar, after strengthening the fort of Calicut, proceeded to Coimbatore. Yet three months had hardly elapsed after his departure, when the Náirs rose in insurrection, and compelled his speedy return.

His lieutenant, Razá Sáhib, marched from Madakkara to suppress the revolt, but was hemmed in by the Náirs, unable either to advance or retreat. Haidar, in spite of the inclemency of the season and the flooded state of the country, advanced boldly into the interior, his troops being exposed to heavy rain, and having frequently to cross the mountain streams up to their chins in water. The Náirs collected their forces in an entrenched camp, and inflicted great loss on the Mysore troops; but a French officer in Haidar's service gallantly led a storming party, which carried the enemy's position, and completely routed them.

Resolved to strike terror into the insurgents, Haidar at first beheaded or hanged all who were taken prisoners, and then resorted to the expedient of deporting the wretched inhabitants wholesale to the plains of Mysore, where thousands of them perished from hunger and misery.

CHAPTER VII

The Maráthás again attack Mysore

In 1766 Rájá Chikka Krishnaráj died. Haidar ordered the Rájá's eldest son Nanjráj to be installed as his nominal successor; but finding on his return to the capital in 1767 that the young chief was inclined to assert his own authority, Haidar confiscated his personal estates, plundered the palace, and assumed entire control over all his household affairs. He could not however but be aware that, by thus virtually declaring himself the ruler of Mysore, he would draw down upon himself active opposition from the Maráthás who had crushed him in 1765; nor was Madhu Ráo tardy in taking steps to overthrow the usurper. A Maráthá coalition was formed with the Nizám for the purpose of invading Mysore, and although Haidar vainly endeavoured to arrest the progress of the Maráthás by despatching Máhfúz Khán, the elder brother of Muhammad Alí, Nawáb of Arcot, to negotiate terms, the Peshwá at the head of his army advanced steadily forward. Haidar resorted to the device of breaking down the embankments of the reservoirs, poisoning the wells, and driving away the miserable peasantry, so as to make the country a waste. But the Peshwá overcame all these obstacles, and reached Sírá, then held by Mír Alí Razá Khán, Haidar's brother-in-law, who treacherously surrendered the fort and deserted Haidar's cause, receiving in reward the district of Gurramkonda. Haidar, alarmed at this betrayal of trust, despatched another envoy in the person of Appají Rám, who by his skilful diplomacy induced the Maráthá chief to withdraw his army on receiving thirty-five lacs of rupees, half of which was paid down, while the Kolár district was pledged for the remainder. Shortly afterwards the balance was paid, and Madhu Ráo returned to his capital at Poona.

CHAPTER VIII

The Nizám joins Haidar Alí, who attacks the English—War from 1767 to 1769

The Peshwá's ally, Nizám Alí, who had been forestalled by the more speedy action of the Maráthás, now appeared on the scene, too late to reap any fruits from the enterprise. Nizám Alí was accompanied by an English corps, but it soon became evident that he contemplated throwing over the compact which he had made with the Madras Government, and allying himself with Haidar, for the purpose of invading the country below the *ghâts*. He succeeded in cajoling the English authorities at Madras by various pretences till the Mysore ruler had made all his preparations. Their combined armies, amounting to 42,860 cavalry, 28,000 infantry, with 109 guns, then descended into the low country, and attacked Colonel Joseph Smith, who was in command of the British troops on the frontier. Haidar at first contented himself with harassing the English by intercepting all supplies, but being urged on by the Nizám, their joint forces attacked Smith near the fort of Changama, where they were repulsed with considerable loss.

Meanwhile Colonel Wood had been ordered to march from Trichinopoli to Trinomalai, where the Arcot Nawáb had assured the Madras Government that ample supplies would be provided. In point of fact hardly anything was procurable there, and the place itself was indefensible. Colonel Smith, after his first encounter with Haidar, proceeded to Trinomalai to furnish himself with ammunition, and effected a junction with Colonel Wood, their united armies comprising 1,030 cavalry, 5,800 infantry, and 16 guns. Haidar and the Nizám now advanced to attack the British troops, taking up a position about six miles from Trinomalai, where Haidar constructed a large redoubt. On Sept. 26, 1767, a hardly-fought contest ensued, which, in spite of their inferior numbers and the desperate charges made by the Mysore cavalry, resulted in a complete victory for the English, the allies losing more than 1.200 killed and 37 guns, while the loss on our side was inconsiderable.

On the cessation of the rainy season, Haidar recaptured Tirupatúr and Vaniambádi, and besieged the strong fort of Ambúr in the Báramaháls, but was gallantly resisted by Captain Calvert, who held out till relieved by a British force sent from Vellúr (Vellore) under the command of Smith. The English then attacked Haidar at Vaniambádi, which he evacuated. Learning however that a convoy with large supplies was on its way to join the English army, Haidar made a desperate attack upon it at Singarapetta, in which he lost several of his officers, and had his horse shot under him, narrowly escaping himself. This failure deterred him from prosecuting further hostilities, while his treacherous ally Nizám Alí, having received information that the English Government had sent a considerable force under Colonel Peach to attack his own territory, was anxious to dissolve connexion with the Mysore chief. He accordingly made secret overtures to the English, and marched northwards, while Haidar, sending his artillery on ahead, accompanied by his son Tipú, reascended the passes, and proceeded westward to secure his possessions on the coast. During his absence in the late campaign, the Náirs of Malabar had shown signs of resistance to his authority, and had received support from the English Government at Bombay, who despatched an expedition to seize Mangalúr (Mangalore). Haidar, leaving Bangalore in charge of his trusty lieutenant Fazl Ullah Khán, marched with all haste to Malabar, and appearing in force before Mangalore captured it with ease, the garrison pusillanimously surrendering the place without opposition, together with their guns, stores, and treasure. Haidar then returned to his headquarters, visiting on his way Bednúr, the landowners of which district had sent supplies to the British, an offence for which he compelled them by means of torture to pay heavy fines.

After the withdrawal of Haidar from the eastern frontier, the Madras Government determined to send troops to reduce all the places seized by him in the

Báramaháls and the country as far south as Dindigal. Fort after fort fell before a column under Colonel Wood, who, having accomplished his part of the work, proceeded to join Colonel Smith. The latter, after attacking the stronghold of Krishnagiri[1], which surrendered, advanced into the Mysore plateau, and took Múlbágal, Kolár, and Hosúr. He was hampered however by the presence of two members of the Madras Council, and was further informed that all arrangements for collecting the revenues of the conquered districts were to be made under the directions or with the assent of Muhammad Alí, the Nawáb of Arcot, whose only object was to secure for himself all the territory wrested from Haidar's clutch. The Madras Government were apparently of opinion that a successful advance might be made on Bangalore, and perhaps on Seringapatam itself. But although the Maráthá chief, Morári Ráo, was induced to join Colonel Smith's force with a fairly strong contingent, the long period of inaction which intervened enabled Haidar to return from his distant expedition to Bangalore and to confront the English before any further steps had been taken. He immediately attacked the Maráthá camp by night, but the onset of his cavalry was defeated by Morári Ráo's strategy. Having been foiled in his attempt, and apprehensive of Bangalore being

[1] Krishnagiri is said to be a virgin fortress, never having been taken, though often attacked. There are numerous other strongholds in India (of which a most interesting account might be written) of far greater strategical importance, but very few which have not succumbed to an enemy by assault.

stormed, he sent off his family and treasure to the rock-fortress of Sávandrúg, a place of great natural strength, twenty-eight miles to the west.

Haidar endeavoured ineffectually to prevent Colonel Wood from joining the force under Colonel Smith, and fled precipitately when the union was accomplished, making his way to Gurramkonda, where he succeeded in inducing his brother-in-law, Alí Razá Khán, to rejoin his standard with his trained troops. Thus reinforced, he returned towards Kolár, but still fearing the probable investment of Bangalore, he made overtures for peace, offering to cede the Báramaháls and pay ten lacs to the British. He declined however to make any concession to Muhammad Alí, whom he thoroughly despised. His offers fell far short of the demands of the Madras delegates, who not only called for the cession of a large territory to their own Government, but also for the payment of tribute to the Nizám. Nothing came therefore of the negotiations, and hostile operations recommenced.

Mention has been made of Múlbágal as one of the places occupied by Colonel Smith. While he was absent, the Madras delegates thought proper to remove his garrison, and to replace them with a company of Muhammad Alí's soldiers. Haidar, on returning from Gurramkonda, won over the commandant and seized the fort, which Colonel Wood at once advanced to recover, being ignorant however that Haidar's army was in the vicinity. Wood succeeded in seizing the lower fort, but the citadel repelled his attempt at an escalade, and the next morning Haidar swooped down upon him with a large body of horse, followed by a heavy column of infantry. A desperate combat ensued, in which Haidar's guns played with great effect, and the English were on the point of being worsted, when Captain Brooke, in command of four companies forming the baggage guard, with great exertion contrived to drag two guns by a concealed path to the top of one of the adjoining rocks[1], from which he opened fire on the enemy, calling out, together with his men, the name of 'Smith.' The Mysoreans, supposing that Colonel Smith had come up to support Colonel Wood, retreated for a time, while Wood was enabled to strengthen his position. Haidar however resumed the attack, and made a desperate charge up the hill with his cavalry, but was driven back with great loss, both sides suffering heavily. Expresses were despatched to Colonel Smith for assistance. Before he could arrive Haidar and his army had disappeared.

It was clear to the English commanders that their force was quite insufficient to capture Bangalore, and that Haidar was not to be drawn into a regular engagement. He was here, there, and everywhere, harassing the enemy with his cavalry, and easily evading pursuit, while he had no hesitation in devastating the country to destroy all supplies of

[1] The configuration of the country in this part of Mysore is remarkable, rocks of every size and shape being tossed about in the wildest confusion. Here also are the auriferous tracts which in recent years have yielded so much gold to European industry.

food. Smith's failure to force him into a general action brought down upon himself however the reproaches of the Madras Government, who had expected him, with insufficient means, in men, ammunition, and provisions, to accomplish the impossible. The futile result was really owing to their own fatuity, want of prescience, and unreasonable confidence in the aid to be rendered by Muhammad Alí. Colonel Smith was directed to repair to Madras, leaving Colonel Wood in command, and Haidar at once commenced to besiege Hosúr. Wood advanced to its relief by way of Báglúr, a few miles distant, leaving there his heavy guns and baggage in charge of Captain Alexander, who commanded a regiment of Muhammad Alí's force. But meanwhile Haidar, relinquishing temporarily the siege of Hosúr, got between Wood and Báglúr, which place he attacked, and, notwithstanding a gallant resistance, succeeded in carrying off Wood's heavy guns and ammunition, and forwarded them to Bangalore. On Wood's retracing his steps, he suddenly found himself overwhelmed by Haidar's army, which drove in his outposts, and commenced a heavy artillery fire that carried destruction into his ranks. These attacks were repeated as he resumed his march, and such was the persistence of the enemy that, with failing ammunition, his native troops began to lose all confidence in their leader, when Major Fitzgerald, who was stationed at Venkatagiri, pushed on to his relief, and averted his entire destruction. The result of this unfortunate enterprise was that Wood was recalled, Colonel Lang being sent to supersede him.

While these abortive attempts were being made to seize Bangalore, Haidar had sent his lieutenant Fazl Ullah Khán to Seringapatam to raise fresh levies of troops, with a view to retaliation on the British. When his preparations were complete, he despatched Fazl Ullah in November, 1768, with a large force down the Gajalhátti Pass to reduce the smaller posts held by the enemy, following himself a month later with the greater part of his army. The resistance encountered by Fazl Ullah Khán was so slight that he had little difficulty in occupying the places referred to, while Haidar, entering the Coimbatore district, seized Karúr and marched towards Erode. On his way thither he was encountered by Captain Nixon, who was under the belief that he was opposed only by Fazl Ullah Khán. Overwhelmed by the immense army launched at him by Haidar, who was in command of 12,000 cavalry and a large body of infantry, Nixon was completely defeated, scarcely a man escaping death or wounds, while Haidar advanced triumphantly on Erode and compelled its surrender. The British officer second in command had capitulated at Vaniambádi in the previous year on condition that he would not serve again during the war, and Haidar, taking advantage of this undoubted breach of honour, sent the whole garrison, as well as that of Káveripuram, which fell shortly afterwards, to languish in prison at Seringapatam. Haidar had now reconquered all the districts south of the *ghâts* which had been wrested from him by the English, and marched eastward towards Madras, a movement which so alarmed the Government there that they despatched Captain Brooke to offer terms of peace.

In the interview which ensued Haidar showed a desire to arrange matters, seeing clearly that the friendship of the British would be more advantageous to him than their hostility. But he resolutely set his face against any concessions to the treacherous and selfish Nawâb of Arcot, who had oppressed and plundered his subjects, and whose exclusion from any arrangement he firmly demanded. As, however, the influence of the Nawâb was predominant in the counsels of the Madras Government, the negotiation was fruitless and hostilities were resumed[1]. Haidar, with that indomitable energy which characterized him, then resorted to an expedient to terrify the authorities at Madras. Sending off the main body of his army with orders to retire westward through the Ahtúr Pass, he himself proceeded eastward, accompanied by 6,000 chosen horse and a very few infantry, and by a forced march of 130 miles reached St. Thomas' Mount, five miles from Madras, in three days and a half.

Here he was practically able to dictate his own terms to the English, and at his suggestion Mr. Du Prè was

[1] Haidar is alleged to have spoken to the envoy as follows: 'I am coming to the gates of Madras, and I will there listen to the propositions the Governor and Council may have to make.'

deputed to meet him. His first demand was for an offensive and defensive alliance, having in view the co-operation of the English in repelling the repeated attacks of the Maráthás on his territory. He did not succeed in carrying his point in this respect, although the Madras Government consented to a stipulation that in case either of the contracting parties should be attacked by other powers, mutual assistance should be rendered to drive the enemy out. The conference ended in an agreement, dated March 29, 1769, for the restoration on both sides of prisoners and places. Among the latter, Karúr, an old possession of Mysore, but then held by Muhammad Alí, was surrendered to Haidar. It cannot be denied that, both in regard to the military operations which preceded this treaty and to the conditions which it embodied, the Mysore chief evinced high qualities as a tactician and the sagacity of a born diplomatist. On the other hand, the proceedings of the Madras Government were characterized by a mixture of rashness and irresolution, and an absurd confidence in their treacherous ally Muhammad Alí, of whose duplicity Haidar had, on the contrary, formed an accurate estimate [1].

[1] A French writer says that, by Haidar's directions, a derisive caricature was affixed to one of the gates of Fort St. George, in which the Governor and his Council were represented as on their knees before Haidar, who held Mr. Du Prè by the nose, drawn in the shape of an elephant's trunk, which poured forth guineas and pagodas. Colonel Smith was shown holding the treaty in his hand, and breaking his sword in two.

CHAPTER IX

THE MARÁTHÁS INVADE MYSORE A FOURTH TIME

HAIDAR had now to prepare for another formidable invasion of Mysore by the Maráthás. Fortified by the tacit assent of Nizám Alí, who viewed with alarm the pretensions of his brother Basálat Jang, Haidar proceeded to levy contributions from the Nawábs of Kadapa and Karnúl, as well as from the smaller chiefs who were subordinate to Sírá. Having thus replenished his treasury, he prepared to oppose the Peshwá's army, demanding also assistance from the English under the provisions of the treaty recently executed. The aid demanded was however never rendered, and Haidar was left alone to bear the brunt of the Maráthá attack. Knowing his inability to meet the foe in the open field, he retreated towards his capital, wasting the country as he retired; but finding his position precarious, he sent an envoy to treat for terms. Madhu Ráo demanded a million (one crore of rupees), partly on account of the exactions levied by Haidar from the chiefs just referred to, and partly as arrears of tribute, which the

Peshwá claimed as being the overlord of Mysore in right of the Maráthá succession to the sovereignty of Bíjapur. These exorbitant demands being rejected by Haidar, Madhu Ráo proceeded to occupy the country, overrunning all the northern and eastern districts, and establishing garrisons at the principal posts. He carried everything before him, but only met with a signal repulse in attacking Nijagal, an almost inaccessible fort about thirty miles north-west of Bangalore. This place, after an investment of three months, was at last taken by the desperate courage of the Pálegár of Chitaldrúg, who, at the head of his brave band of Bedars, succeeded in seizing the fortress by escalade. Madhu Ráo ordered the noses and ears of all the survivors of the garrison to be cut off, the only man who escaped mutilation being the commandant, Sardár Khán, whose undaunted behaviour before the Peshwá secured him immunity.

Madhu Ráo, whose movements had been attended with entire success, now fell ill and returned to Poona, leaving his maternal uncle Trimbak Ráo in command[1]. This chief, after reducing Gurramkonda, returned to the west, conquering several districts not yet seized by his nephew; but in the meanwhile Haidar had assembled a large force of cavalry and infantry, with

[1] Trimbak Ráo was a son of Hari Bhatt, the progenitor of the Patwardhan family, which was allied by marriage to the Peshwá, and, though Bráhmans by caste, gave many commanders to the Maráthá armies, especially Parasu Rám Bháo, who became notorious for the ruthless devastations which he committed in Mysore and the adjoining territory.

which he determined to stay the invasion of his territory.

There is a sacred shrine called Melukote about twenty miles north of Seringapatam. Haidar, after some ineffectual manœuvres near the stupendous rock-fortress of Sávandrúg, entered the eastern pass leading into the hills within which Melukote is situated, and drew up his troops in the form of a crescent facing the west, with his flanks resting on the most inaccessible sides of the hills. There happened however to be a detached hill on the eastern approach, from which the Maráthás during eight days kept up a galling cannonade. To this, Haidar, having no large guns, was unable to reply, and his position became at length so intolerable that he resolved to retire on Seringapatam by the southern pass of the hills. His troops marched at night, but Haidar, having drunk freely in the evening, was not in a fit state to superintend the movement, while his son Tipú was nowhere to be found[1], and the accidental firing off of a gun apprised the Maráthás that the Mysore army was in retreat. An immediate pursuit was ordered, and the Maráthá cavalry, aided by some guns which were brought to bear upon the enemy with great effect from the banks of a reservoir called the Pearl Tank, hovered in swarms about Haidar's infantry, which with much difficulty reached the hills near Chirkúli, or Chinkuráli. Here the utmost confusion ensued,

[1] Haidar is said to have personally chastised Tipú for this breach of duty.

and during the panic the Maráthá horse charged the fugitives, and breaking through the square which had been formed, commenced an indiscriminate slaughter. Seeing that all was lost, and that the enemy were engaged in plundering his camp, Haidar escaped alone and unattended to Seringapatam, a distance of eleven miles, and was soon after followed by Tipú in the disguise of a fakír or mendicant. The only officer who behaved gallantly on the occasion was Fazl Ullah Khán, who, cutting his way through the enemy, with a small body of men, forded the Káveri and reached Seringapatam in safety. This disastrous affair occurred on March 5, 1771.

Melukote, being a richly-endowed shrine and the headquarters of the sect of Srí Váishnava Bráhmans, offered an irresistible allurement to the greed of the Maráthás, and as the place was deserted they did not hesitate, after pillaging the precincts, to set fire to the temple cars, which involved the destruction of the sacred buildings. The delay caused by the inveterate habit of plundering which characterized the Maráthás enabled Haidar to take measures for the effectual defence of his capital, which Trimbak Ráo besieged with no result. The Maráthá host continued however to hold the greater part of his territory for more than a year. Haidar, despairing of getting rid of the enemy, then sued for peace, which was concluded in June, 1772, on his agreeing to pay at once fifteen lacs, and a like sum afterwards, some of his richest districts being given in pledge. During the course of these hostilities Haidar discovered that the young Rájá Nanjráj had been in secret communication with the Maráthás, whereupon he ruthlessly ordered him to be strangled, substituting for him his brother Chámráj.

CHAPTER X

Conquest of Coorg

Relieved from the pressure imposed upon him by the Maráthás, Haidar began to recruit his means by exacting heavy contributions from all the wealthy persons he could seize. On hearing of the dissensions at Poona as to the succession, on the death of the Peshwá Náráyan Ráo [1], he despatched Tipú to regain possession of the territory ceded to the Maráthás, while he himself prepared to recover Malabar. Between the Mysore country and Malabar intervenes the small mountainous district of Coorg—now the field of active European enterprise in the production of coffee,—and as its subjugation appeared to Haidar to be essential to his keeping open his communication with the coast, he suddenly entered the country towards the end of 1773.

Coorg, or Kodagú, is a most picturesque alpine region, heavily wooded, and bounded on the west by

[1] Náráyan Ráo succeeded his brother Madhu Ráo in 1772, but was treacherously murdered in the ensuing year, at the instigation of his uncle Raghubá, who then claimed the succession, to the exclusion of a posthumous son of Náráyan Ráo, named Madhu Ráo Náráyan.

the great chain of Ghâts, which look down upon Malabar. It is inhabited by a sturdy and warlike race, the headmen living each on his own farm homestead, surrounded by the dwellings of his kinsmen, and his agrestic labourers, who were formerly serfs. By religion the Coorg Rájás were Lingáyats, and the word Bráhman stank in their nostrils. The mass of the people worshipped the sylvan deities, to whom many of the finest forests in the country were dedicated. The Coorgs appear to have maintained their independence, only acknowledging the jurisdiction of their own local chiefs, till the early part of the seventeenth century, when a scion of the Ikkeri house, previously mentioned, settled in the country as a devotee, and gradually obtained an ascendancy over the people, who made him yearly offerings, and consented to guard his person by sending relays of watchmen. In the course of a few years he felt himself sufficiently strong to declare himself ruler of Háleri and the surrounding districts; and somewhat later all the headmen acknowledged him as their chief, agreeing to pay him one-quarter of their rentals.

When Haidar seized Bednúr in 1763 he affected to regard Coorg as tributary to that principality, and in 1765 sent a force to reduce the country, but was foiled in his attempt. In 1770 a dispute broke out in Coorg as to the succession. Lingaráj, uncle of one of the claimants, sought the aid of Haidar, who was only too ready to promise his support. The Maráthá invasion had caused Haidar to suspend his designs, but as soon as he had got rid of his powerful enemy, he proceeded with a large force to Coorg, and intriguing with both sides, succeeded in reaching Merkára, the capital, with little opposition [1]. Devappa, the antagonist of the claimant whose cause Haidar had espoused, fled, but was shortly afterwards seized and sent to Seringapatam, where he died in prison. Haidar, having attained his object, at once despatched a force through Wainád to Calicut, and speedily achieved the re-conquest of the whole of Malabar.

[1] Some authorities state that on his first appearance on the frontier Haidar offered a reward of five rupees for the head of every Coorg which was brought to him, and that 700 heads were in consequence delivered. This account may be true, and is paralleled by the conduct of General Avitabile, who, when in command at Peshávar, actually gave a grant of two villages to a leader of cavalry on condition that he brought in yearly the heads of fifty Afrídís. The writer has a copy of this assignment of land.

CHAPTER XI

NEGOTIATIONS WITH RAGHUBÁ—DEATH OF MYSORE RÁJÁ—CAPTURE OF BELLARY AND GÚTTI—ATTITUDE OF THE POONA MINISTRY

WHILE engaged in re-establishing his authority on the coast, Haidar ordered Tipú to recover the districts wrested from him by the Maráthás. This was accomplished by the beginning of 1774, after which he took advantage of the doubtful position in which Raghubá, or Raghunáth Ráo, stood, to offer his co-operation and acknowledge him as the rightful Peshwá on condition that the tribute payable by Mysore should be reduced to six lacs. The elevation of Raghubá was vehemently opposed by the famous Bálájí Janárdhan, commonly called Náná Farnavis, the finance minister of Madhu Ráo, who supported the superior claims of Náráyan Ráo's posthumous son, and was afterwards a determined opponent of British influence. But Haidar cared little who was the rightful heir, and thought the opportunity favourable for securing his own interests.

Shortly afterwards a serious insurrection broke out

in Coorg, owing to the oppressive exactions of the Bráhman officials whom Haidar had appointed to collect the revenue, and whom the people of the country cordially detested. The landholders rose in every direction, and invested Merkára, but Haidar marched a strong force immediately into the province, and suppressed the rebellion with little difficulty, hanging without remorse all its leaders.

In 1776 the young Rájá Chámráj died. Haidar adopted the strange expedient of collecting together all the young scions of the house, and then throwing before them a variety of playthings and ornaments, watched the result. One of the children, named also Chámráj, attracted by the glitter of a jewelled dagger, seized it in one hand and with the other grasped a lime, whereupon Haidar facetiously remarked that that was the real Rájá, and accordingly ordered him to be installed as the future ruler[1].

Haidar's next expedition was to succour the Pálegár of Bellary, on the north-east frontier of Mysore; that chief having renounced his allegiance to Basálat Jang, who despatched a corps under M. Lally to besiege him. Haidar, marching with the extraordinary celerity which distinguished all his movements, reached Bellary in five days. He completely surprised the attacking party, and immediately seized the fort, which was unconditionally surrendered to him, while Lally

[1] This boy was the father of the late Mahárájá Krishnaráj, who, after a long rule of sixty-eight years, died at a venerable age in 1868, having been put on the throne of his ancestors in 1799.

escaped with difficulty. He then proceeded to demand a heavy contribution from Morári Ráo of Gútti, sixty miles to the eastward. On that chief refusing, he besieged the place, but although he succeeded in capturing the lower fort, where he secured a large booty, the upper citadel[1], which was virtually impregnable, resisted all his efforts to take it. Owing to the great numbers of followers who were in the fort, the garrison began to be in want of water, and Morári Ráo, concealing the fact, was anxious to come to an arrangement. But Haidar, having skilfully elicited from his envoy the distress to which his chief was reduced, protracted the negotiations till Morári Ráo in despair was obliged to surrender with all his troops. Haidar, besides levying a contribution of ten lacs, annexed the adjacent territory, and sent the whole family to Seringapatam, whence Morári Ráo was afterwards despatched to the fatal rock of Kabáldrúg[2], where he died.

In March, 1775, Raghubá had succeeded in inducing the Bombay Government to support his cause. Strengthened by this alliance, he proposed to Haidar

[1] The citadel was on the summit of a huge smooth rock of granite, on the north side of a circular cluster of hill fortifications, all of which it overlooked.

[2] This fortified hill is of conical shape, and is about 4,000 feet above the sea. The ascent is extremely steep and slippery, steps being cut in the solid rock to afford a sufficient hold to the feet. There is water on the summit, as in the case of nearly all the Mysore *drúgs*, but it is most unwholesome, so that this circumstance, added to its isolated position in the south of the province, made the fortress a convenient state prison. One of the Mysore Rájás died while confined here.

to occupy all the Maráthá possessions up to the river Krishna, a plan which the Mysore ruler lost no time in carrying out, seizing nearly half this territory before the advent of the rainy season compelled him to return to Seringapatam[1].

The result of this coalition was that the Poona ministers and Nizám Alí declared war against Haidar. They despatched a large force to dislodge him from the Sávanúr country, while a still larger army was equipped for further operations. Their advance force was, however, skilfully defeated at Sáunsi, ten miles north of Sávanúr, by Haidar's general, Muhammad Alí. By a feigned flight, he inveigled the Maráthás into a rash pursuit, which brought them under the fire of the Mysore guns, and caused great confusion in their ranks. Then Muhammad Alí, making a determined charge with his cavalry, utterly routed them, capturing two of their leaders, and inflicting great slaughter. Meanwhile the main army of the Maráthás under Parasu Rám Bháo was advancing from Poona, while Nizám Alí had despatched a force of 40,000 men under Ibráhím Khán to co-operate from the eastward. The former, however, hearing of the decisive victory ob-

[1] Dhárwár, the capital of this territory, was taken by an ingenious stratagem. A fictitious letter was sent to the commandant telling him that aid was coming to him from the Maráthás. Haidar then dressed up some of his troops in the guise of Maráthás and directed another detachment to attack them, and fire at them with blank cartridges. The garrison, believing that the first-named body constituted the expected relief, admitted them into the fort, when they seized the commandant, disarmed the defenders of the place, and took possession of it for Haidar.

tained by Muhammad Alí, hesitated to advance, and applied for reinforcements, retiring beyond the Krishna, while the Nizám's general, who had proceeded as far as Adoni on the way to Gútti, Haidar's headquarters, either fearing an encounter or being bribed by his adversary, also judged it expedient to withdraw within the Nizám's territory. The rainy season now set in and prevented any further military operations on either side.

CHAPTER XII

Siege of Chitaldrúg—Operations against the Maráthás—Reduction of Chitaldrúg

Haidar availed himself of this respite to punish the defection of the Pálegár of Chitaldrúg, who had failed to send his contingent to support him in the recent contest. It will be remembered that on the invasion of Madhu Ráo, this Pálegár had distinguished himself in the assault of the Nijagal fort, then held by Haidar, who never forgave him for this gallant feat, and was determined to compel his unconditional submission.

The clan of Bedars, of which the Pálegár Madakeri Náyak was the chief, is said to have migrated from Jádíkaldrúg in Kadapa, some marches west of the famous shrine of Tirupati, and to have settled in the neighbourhood of Chitaldrúg in the year 1475. Their leader, named Timmana, was appointed by the King of Vijayanagar to the office of Náyak of Chitaldrúg, and his son Obana, on the fall of Vijayanagar in 1564, assumed independence. The Bedars gradually extended their possessions, which eventually yielded a revenue of four or five lacs, but during the rule of Barmappa Náyak, the *páliam* became tributary to the Mughal deputy at Sírá. As Haidar had seized that district, which the Maráthás also claimed as an appanage of the Bíjapur Kingdom, the Náyak felt himself to be in a precarious position, both parties demanding his allegiance. He was at the same time conscious of the natural strength of Chitaldrúg and of the fidelity of his clan. The town was built at the base of a mass of rugged desolate hills extending many miles west and south; and was girt by an extensive line of fortifications, which, when manned by the brave Bedars, offered a formidable resistance to Haidar's attacks. The siege was protracted for three months, the defenders constantly sallying out, and carrying back the heads of Haidar's soldiers as a propitiatory sacrifice to the goddess Káli. On hearing that a vast Maráthá force was rapidly approaching his frontier, Haidar had to content himself with a handsome sum as ransom, and the evasive promise of the Pálegár to join his standard in future.

The Maráthá host was commanded by Hari Panth Pharkia, and comprised 60,000 horse, with a due proportion of infantry and guns. After waiting for some time for the Nizám's force, they crossed the Tungábhadra, and encamped at Raravi, where Haidar advanced to meet them. He had previously bribed Mánáji Pánkria, an influential leader, to abandon Hari Panth at the decisive moment, and draw off his troops. But this chief wavering as to his course of action, Haidar directed demonstrations to be made in the shape of pretended communications with him, which inspired

Hari Panth with a conviction of his treachery, and induced him to attack the recreant leader, who was overwhelmed by a mass of cavalry and driven off the field. Hari Panth then retired across the river, effecting his retreat in good order, but harassed by incessant assaults from the army of Haidar, who proceeded to seize all the territory between the Tungábhadra and the Krishna, reducing the strongholds of Kopal and Gajendragarh, with minor posts, and capturing Dhárwár after a long siege. All the local chiefs then tendered their submission, and having completed his dispositions for the permanent occupation of the country, Haidar returned to Mysore in 1779 to wreak his vengeance on the Pálegár of Chitaldrúg, who had failed to co-operate with him in the recent struggle. The chief made a gallant resistance, but having in his service 3,000 Musalmán soldiers, Haidar found means to corrupt them through the agency of a holy fakír who resided near the town. Madakeri Náyak, finding that he was betrayed, was obliged to throw himself on the mercy of Haidar, who, after plundering the place, despatched the Pálegár and his family to languish in prison at Seringapatam. Haidar was determined to make short work of the brave Bedars who had so successfully fought against him, and heroically sacrificed their lives in defending their hereditary chief. Not content with confiscating all their available property, and ravaging the district for the support of his army, he carried off to his capital 20,000 of the inhabitants. The young boys were afterwards trained to arms, and formed the first nucleus of a band of compulsory converts from Hinduism to Islám; a band which was largely augmented in the reign of Tipú Sultán, under the title of the Chela, or disciple battalions [1].

[1] The kind-hearted but simple missionary, Schwartz, when he visited Seringapatam in 1779, was led to believe that these boys were destitute orphans, whom Haidar had kindly taken under his protection.

CHAPTER XIII

ANNEXATION OF KADAPA—HAIDAR'S DRACONIAN RULE—ROYAL MARRIAGES

WHILE engaged in the above enterprise, Haidar had despatched his brother-in-law, Alí Razá Khán, called Mír Sáhib, to enforce the submission of the Nawáb of Kadapa, Abd-ul-Halím Khán. The latter had, in the contest with the Maráthás, abjured the cause of Haidar and served with the Nizám, but Mír Sáhib failed to subdue the hardy Afgháns, who resolutely opposed him. Haidar, when the siege of Chitaldrúg was at an end, proceeded by forced marches to his assistance, and on reaching Dhúr, north of Kadapa, came in contact with the Afghán cavalry. These, finding themselves attacked by the whole of Haidar's horse, retreated to the town in good order, but being completely surrounded, were compelled to surrender. Haidar was only too glad to take into his service such of this brave band as could obtain securities for their allegiance, but among them were eighty troopers whose horses had been killed, and who could not find any one to be surety for them. They refused to be disarmed, and Haidar, respecting their feelings, did not enforce the surrender of their weapons. Afgháns, however, as he must have well known, are an eminently treacherous race. The eighty troopers, smarting under the disgrace to which he had proposed to subject them, rose in the dead of night, overpowered and killed the guards placed over them, and penetrated to the tent of Haidar, who, disturbed by the noise, made up the semblance of a person asleep with a pillow, cut a hole through his tent, and succeeded in escaping. On the alarm being given most of the assassins were slain. Such of them as survived had their hands and feet chopped off, while a few were killed by being dragged round the camp, attached to the feet of elephants [1]. The Nawáb had fled to Sidháut, a short distance to the east of Kadapa, but surrendered shortly afterwards, on a guarantee being given for his personal security. He was despatched to Seringapatam with the rest of his family, but his beautiful sister was compelled to marry the destroyer of her house, who placed her at the head of his harem with the title of Bakshí Begam [2].

[1] This was a not uncommon mode of punishing malefactors. A more recent instance is the murder of Etojí, brother of Jaswant Ráo Holkar, who was barbarously killed in this fashion by the Peshwá Bájí Ráo in 1799.

[2] The heads of many of the State departments were styled 'Bakshí,' literally meaning dispensers, but technically controllers, so that this appellation probably signifies Controller of the Women's department—no doubt a responsible post, for Haidar, though perhaps not susceptible in the higher sense to the charms of female beauty and never allowing any woman to influence his public actions, was a man of the loosest morals, and never spared any one of the sex

Haidar's authority being now firmly established, he commenced a scrutiny into the several departments of the State. He appointed Mír Muhammad Sádik his minister of finance, and Shámáiya his head of police, with full powers, not only to prevent crime, but to extract by force, and even torture, the substance of all the wealthy men who came under his observation. Nor did this Bráhman hesitate to avail himself of the foulest means to extort money for the service of his patron. Flogging was freely resorted to in order to mulct the revenue officials of their ill-gained accumulations, while all the bankers in the country were forced to pay heavy contributions for State expenses. Even the troops did not escape Haidar's exactions, inasmuch as he gradually introduced a system of payment called the *das máhi*, or ten months' pay in the year instead of twelve. The mounted troops, who horsed themselves, were paid for only twenty days in the month, the balance being supposed to be made up by the plunder which they were allowed to retain at Haidar's own valuation.

Having crushed the Kadapa Nawáb, Haidar next sought to attach the Sávanúr Nawáb, Abd-ul-Hakím, to his interests by a nuptial alliance; and, in accordance with his suggestions, that chief's eldest son married Haidar's daughter, while Abd-ul-Hakím's daughter was married to Karím, Tipú's brother. The tribute payable by the Nawáb was reduced by one

who had the misfortune to attract his attention. Bakshi Begam's tomb is at Vellore.

half, on his agreeing to furnish 2,000 troopers for Haidar's service. All these arrangements were carried out to Haidar's satisfaction, and the marriage ceremonies were conducted, in 1779, with pomp and magnificence at Seringapatam in the presence of the two chiefs.

CHAPTER XIV

COMBINATION OF THE MARÁTHÁS AND THE NIZÁM WITH HAIDAR AGAINST THE ENGLISH—FRUITLESS NEGOTIATIONS

DURING the progress of these festivities an ambassador named Ganésh Ráo arrived at Haidar's capital with proposals from the Poona Darbár that he should join the Maráthás and the Nizám in expelling the English from Southern India. The history of the complicated transactions which led to this design will show to the unprejudiced reader, on the one hand the moderation of Haidar, and on the other the perfidy of the Nawáb of Arcot and the weakness of the Madras Government.

It may be remembered that in March, 1775, the Bombay Government had made a treaty with Raghubá, in which they agreed to support his pretensions. But it soon became apparent that the great mass of the Maráthá nation, including the powerful chiefs, Sindhia and Holkar, were adverse to his rule, being stimulated in their opposition by the astute policy of Náná Farnavis, who, it is alleged, desired to supplant in his own person the family of the Peshwá.

It is not proposed to discuss here the evil results, terminating in the disgraceful convention of Wargám, which arose from the ill-considered measures of the Bombay Government. It suffices to say that the Maráthá nation had good cause to be dissatisfied with the action of the British authorities, who had attempted to force upon them, as a ruler, one whose ascendancy was repudiated by all the influential chiefs of their race.

The Nizám had also his grievances, which inclined him to co-operate with the Maráthás and Haidar. On the occupation of the Sarkárs, or the coast region of the Madras Presidency on the Bay of Bengal, one of these districts, that is, Guntúr, was granted as a jágír to Basálat Jang, with the assent of his brother Nizám Alí, the ruling Nizám. Some years afterwards Basálat Jang took into his service a force of French troops, whom he declined to disband, while the Nizám, on being applied to, refused to interfere. In 1778, when war with France seemed imminent, the Madras Government availed themselves of the agency of Muhammad Alí of Arcot to enter into negotiations with Basálat Jang, ignoring his suzerain, the Nizám. The result was that Basálat Jang ceded the district for a certain rental, and dismissed his French troops, on condition that the English Government agreed to defend him against the attacks of Haidar on Adoni. No sooner had the Madras Government acquired possession of Guntúr, than they leased it to Muhammad Alí. This was unquestionably an invasion of the rights of the

Nizám, for, although the Company were to enjoy the reversion of the district on Basálat Jang's death, the Nizám was during his lifetime the actual suzerain of the territory. Irritated by this contemptuous disregard of his rights, Nizám Alí was justified in stating to the English Resident who was despatched to his Court that, in acting as they had done, the Madras Government had set aside the treaty made with him. His indignation knew no bounds when he ascertained from the same envoy that they purposed also to ignore in future the payment of the tribute which, on the cession of the Sarkárs by the emperor, the British Government had weakly consented to pay to the Nizám.

Haidar on his part had still greater reason to complain of the manner in which he had been treated by the Madras authorities. In all his struggles with the Maráthás, he had been studiously denied that co-operation and support which our treaty made with him in 1769 had apparently assured to him, while all his endeavours to effect a friendly alliance with the English had been thwarted by the evil influence of the Arcot Nawáb, who, for his own aggrandizement, had kept open the breach between Haidar and the Madras Government. In 1767 the Arcot Nawáb had sent an agent to England with instructions to bring about a direct intercourse with the British Government, independently of the authorities at Madras—a proceeding which has in later times been pursued by other Indian potentates with evil results.

In compliance with his solicitations, Sir John Lindsay was deputed from London to his court, with full powers to act, irrespectively of the Madras Government. The latter found themselves hampered in their action when this delegate insisted on their joining the Maráthás and Muhammad Alí in crushing Haidar, with whom they had a mutual defensive alliance. It redounds to the credit of Haidar Alí that, when the Maráthás proposed, in 1771, to settle their differences with him by an engagement that he should assist them in subjugating the eastern provinces, he made known their proposals to the English authorities. He frankly stated his opinion that such a union would give the Maráthás so predominant an influence that it would seriously imperil eventually his own position, and added that, if his alliance were rejected by the Madras Government, he should have no alternative but to seek assistance from the French. In 1773 he renewed his endeavours to procure a treaty, but his proposals were again frustrated by the insidious policy of Muhammad Alí, who, while urging the English to decline Haidar's advances, was at the same time assuring that chief of his anxious desire to see them driven out of India. With this professed object, he even sent an embassy the next year to Seringapatam to beguile Haidar into a conviction of his sincerity. But Haidar was not to be deceived by his false protestations, and dismissed his envoys in contempt after they had been many months in Mysore. From this date Haidar abandoned all hopes of contracting a firm alliance with the English, and, although he maintained a semblance of friendship for a time, he felt that his own security necessitated his seeking support elsewhere. Animated by these feelings, he entered into correspondence with M. Bellecombe, the French Governor of Pondicherry, who, foreseeing an opportunity of restoring the prestige of his nation in India, readily furnished him with stores and ammunition, and promised him assistance. Haidar still hesitated however, before coming to an open rupture with us, and peace might have been preserved but for certain events which excited his indignation.

On war breaking out between England and France. Pondicherry was captured from the French after a gallant resistance in 1778, and in March of the ensuing year, Mahé[1], on the Malabar coast, also fell before the British troops. Haidar, who was in possession of the whole of Malabar, except the few places occupied by European settlements, was enraged at the seizure of Mahé, which he alleged to be under his protection. His soldiers had in fact assisted in its defence. His main objection to its occupation by the English was that through Mahé he derived his military supplies, and he threatened the British Government that, in the event of Mahé being attacked, he would retaliate by invading Arcot. The capture of the settlement led to an uprising of the Náirs, who were anxious to throw off Haidar's yoke, but the rebellion

[1] This small French settlement has an area of only five square miles, with a population of 8,400, and is subordinate to Pondicherry.

was suppressed without difficulty. Another cause of offence arose in this way. When Basálat Jang, as above mentioned, made over to the Madras Government the district of Guntúr, he requested them to despatch troops to occupy it, and a detachment was accordingly directed to proceed to Adoni by way of Kadapa, at that time under Haidar's jurisdiction, and then on through Karnúl to Guntúr. No permission had been obtained, either from Haidar or the Nizám, for the troops to pass through their territories, the commanding officer being merely furnished with a recommendatory letter from the Madras Governor. The detachment was attacked in a rugged defile and compelled to retreat, and, although reinforcements were sent in haste from Madras, Haidar had meanwhile despatched troops, which ravaged the whole country up to Adoni and stopped any further advance. He was aware of the intention of the Madras Government to lease Guntúr to his enemy, Muhammad Alí. The Nizám for his part was equally opposed to the district being removed from his authority by the compact between his brother, Basálat Jang, and the British authorities at Madras.

This last occurrence took place just at the time when Sir Thomas Rumbold, the Governor, had entrusted the missionary, Schwartz, with a secret embassy to Haidar, who, resenting the conduct of the British in seizing Mahé, had written in strong terms to Madras complaining of their hostility, and intimating the probable consequences. Schwartz was received with cordiality, however, and Haidar expatiated fully on the actual state of affairs, speaking without reserve of preceding events, and expressing his wish to maintain friendly relations if possible. In writing to the Governor, on the missionary's taking leave, he recalled all that had passed—dwelling on the violation of the treaty of 1769, the treacherous behaviour of Muhammad Alí, the rejection of his own offers for peace, and the hostile attitude evinced towards him by the two occurrences just related. His communications were straightforward, and placed all the facts of the case in the clearest possible light, but the Madras Government neither promised reparation, nor adopted adequate means of defence against the threatened invasion of their territory. Immediately after Schwartz's mission, another was despatched to Seringapatam to demand the release of some Englishmen, who had been seized at Calicut, and sent as prisoners to the capital. Mr. Gray, the envoy, was empowered not only to effect their freedom, but to attempt to resume friendly relations. The prisoners were in fact released before he entered Mysore, but, on his proceeding to Seringapatam, Haidar's attitude showed clearly that in his opinion the time for negotiation was passed. After reproaching the English Government for their want of faith, and rejecting all the proposals urged by their envoy, the latter was permitted to depart, having been studiously insulted, and treated rather as a spy than an ambassador.

CHAPTER XV

HAIDAR DECLARES WAR AGAINST THE ENGLISH—HIS INVASION OF MADRAS TERRITORY, AND MILITARY OPERATIONS UP TO HIS DEATH

HAIDAR had at length resolved on war, and on carrying out, so far as he was concerned, the conditions laid before him by the Maráthá envoy, Ganesh Ráo. These prescribed mutual co-operation on the part of the Maráthás, the Nizám, and Haidar, the last to be confirmed in possession of the territory held by him north of the Tungábhadra, while the tribute payable by him in future was to be fixed at 11 lacs. The general scheme of the confederacy was, that the Maráthás should invade Berár, Central and Northern India, while Nizám Alí undertook the subjugation of the Sarkárs, and Haidar Alí that of the Madras territory and Southern India. The coalition was a formidable one, and, when aided by the French, threatened the very existence of the British power in India.

Haidar now began his preparations for this invasion which he had so long contemplated. Having made due provision for the protection of all the principal posts in Mysore, he assembled his army at Bangalore, where he mustered 83,000 men[1], a force which, in regard to efficiency, if not strength, surpassed any previously collected in Southern India. His system of maintaining scouts and spies was perfect, the commissariat under Púrnaiya was well organized, and every precaution was taken to ensure success, not omitting the customary religious ceremonies. Having gathered his forces at the heads of the passes, and issued his instructions to the commanders of the several columns, he suddenly, in July, 1780, swept down upon the plains like an avalanche, carrying destruction with him.

Muhammad Alí had warned the Madras Government of the intended invasion, although, beyond mere professions of fidelity to their cause, he had furnished neither money nor troops to assist them. His rapacity made him chary of proffering aid in the former shape, while his soldiers were in a state of mutiny owing to deferred pay. Haidar moreover had kept his secret well, while the Madras Council, having no proper intelligence department, had no means of penetrating his designs, and it was not

[1] The detail given by Wilks is as follows:—

Stable horse	14,000
Sillahdár horse	12,000
Sávanúr Contingent	2,000
Infantry Disciplined	15,000
Veteran Peons	12,000
Selections from local establishments	18,000
Peons of Pálegárs	10,000
	83,000

till burning villages in the vicinity of St. Thomas' Mount, nine miles from Madras, betrayed his devastating course, that they began to prepare for defence. Haidar's scheme was to lay waste all the country from the Pulicat Lake down to Pondicherry for a considerable distance inland, thus isolating Fort St. George, and preventing any aid coming from the north and west, while he anticipated co-operation himself from the French on the coast-line.

Alarmed at the danger which threatened them, the Madras Government directed Colonel Harper, then in command of the Guntúr detachment, to proceed at once southward. Colonel Braithwaite was also ordered to move from Pondicherry on Madras by way of Chingalpat, and a force from Trichinopoli was instructed to intercept the communications of the enemy through the passes leading to the Báramahâls. As no confidence could be placed in Muhammad Alí, detachments were despatched to occupy the forts of Wodiarpáliam, Jinjí, Karnátikgarh, and Wándiwásh, then held by his troops. The first of these expeditions was for a time successful, and Lieutenant Flint with great address secured possession of the fortress of Wándiwásh, which he continued to hold for six months with skill and resolution. The other two enterprises proved abortive.

Haidar, having descended through the Báramahâls and the Changama Pass, detached a force under his son Karím to attack Porto Novo, south of Pondicherry. He himself proceeded to invest Arcot, but hearing of the movement of the British troops under Sir Hector Munro, he abandoned the siege on August 29. On the same day the Madras Commander-in-Chief reached Conjevaram, which he found denuded of supplies, and there awaited the arrival of the Guntúr force, commanded by Colonel Baillie. This officer reached the Cortelár on August 25, encamping by mistake on the left bank instead of the right; and a sudden fall of rain coming on, the river became so swollen that his crossing was impeded till September 4. On the 6th, Haidar despatched Tipú with the flower of his army to cut off the detachment on its way to Perambákam, while he remained himself near Conjevaram watching Sir Hector Munro. Tipú's attacks were, however, bravely repulsed by Baillie's handful of troops, and on the 9th a force under Colonel Fletcher, numbering 1,000 men, which had been detached by Munro from the main army, succeeded, fortunately without interruption from the enemy, in joining him.

The same night Baillie left Perambákam on his way to Conjevaram. He had not proceeded far before the enemy's guns opened on his rear. An attempt was made to seize these guns, but the flooded state of the ground, which was intersected by ditches, offered a serious impediment. The difficulty was overcome, however, and the enemy's artillery silenced, when Colonel Baillie, contrary to the advice of Colonel Fletcher, determined to halt for the rest of the night, instead of continuing his march to join Munro, then only nine miles off. This delay enabled Tipú to remove his guns to a strong post by which the English had to pass, while Haidar was not slow to take advantage of so favourable an opportunity.

On September 10, the force of 3,700 men commenced their march, but had not proceeded more than two miles when six guns opened on their rear, and large bodies of Haidar's cavalry appeared on their flanks. It was evident that Haidar's whole army was upon them. A detachment of ten companies of Grenadiers under Captains Rumley and Gowdie gallantly stormed and took four of Tipú's guns, but the rapid approach of an immense body of horse, which Haidar had pushed forward to prevent their rejoining the English force, caused great confusion among the Sepoys. Haidar now brought his guns into action, while his numerous cavalry, supported by his infantry, and led by his ablest officers, bore down upon the small English army, without, however, making much impression, so gallant was the resistance. Haidar was discouraged, and inclined to retreat, but the inadvisability of such a course was strongly pressed upon him by M. Lally, who pointed to the probable appearance of Munro on the field. In the meanwhile Tipú had collected his troops together and renewed his cannonade, his guns, with those of Haidar, numbering more than fifty. Two of the English tumbrels were blown up, and their ammunition falling short, Baillie could only reply with grape. While they were in this condition, Haidar charged with the main body of his cavalry, and his infantry poured in volleys with great effect. Baillie, though badly wounded, rallied the Europeans, and forming them into a square, gained an eminence, whence he repulsed thirteen attacks of the enemy, but fresh bodies of cavalry pouring in, his line was at last broken. The Europeans bravely maintained their reputation for intrepidity, but a panic seized the Sepoys and Colonel Baillie was compelled to ask for quarter. His flag of truce was, however, disregarded, as some of our native troops still kept up an irregular fire, and when the order to lay down arms was given, the enemy rushed in and slaughtered deliberately all whom they encountered. Had it not been for the humane interposition of Lally and a French officer named Pimorin, it is probable that not a man would have escaped. Even as it was, 700 Europeans were killed[1]. Haidar is said to have sat in state after the battle to distribute rewards for the production of prisoners, and to enjoy the sight of the heads of the slain. Of those who were captured none were released; some of them died, and others were put to death. This disaster was the most fatal that had ever overtaken the British arms in India, and was commemorated at Seringapatam by an elaborate painting on the walls of the Daryá Dáulat Garden, where it is still to be seen.

[1] French authorities allege that 2,000 English were taken prisoners with Baillie, and 5,000 Sepoys killed, together with the 700 Europeans mentioned above. Among the captives was the gallant Baird (afterwards Sir David Baird), who remained in confinement more than three years. There is a story that his mother, knowing his intractable temper, remarked that 'she pitied the man who was chained to our Davie.'

It was a fortunate thing that British interests in India had at this time been confided to Warren Hastings, and that his master spirit controlled their destiny. The penetration of this great statesman had foreseen the emergency which had arisen, and the vigorous steps which it was essential to take to restore the reputation and prestige of the British Government.

Sir Eyre Coote, whose distinguished services in 1757 had gained him a high reputation, and whose brilliant career subsequently, when opposed to the French in Southern India two years later, had added greatly to his fame, and won for him the attachment of the native troops under him, was now commanding in Bengal. He was nearly sixty years old, and no longer possessed his former bodily strength. But his mental faculties were unimpaired, and Hastings perceived at once that his great military experience would be invaluable in the crisis which had arisen. At the request of the Governor-General, Sir Eyre Coote proceeded to Madras, where he arrived early in November, being entrusted with full powers to prosecute the war. Meanwhile, Haidar, after Baillie's defeat, had recommenced the siege of Arcot, and aided by the skill of the French engineers in his service, who effected two breaches in the walls, took the fort by assault after a severe conflict, in which Tipú's column suffered heavily. He was less successful, however, in his attempts to reduce the other forts of the English. All of them held out, except Ambúr, and Sir Eyre Coote having relieved Chingalpat and occupied Karangúli, proceeded to the assistance of Lieutenant Flint, who still maintained his position at Wándiwásh, notwithstanding repeated attempts on the part of Haidar to dislodge him. Coote's advance was opportune, as Flint's supply of ammunition was exhausted. The enemy lost heart and abandoned the siege, Coote having the satisfaction of knowing that he had raised a second time the siege of a place which he had relieved twenty-one years before.

The sudden appearance of a French fleet off Madras made it impossible for him to receive supplies by sea, or to move to the north, so after relieving Permakoil, he moved towards Pondicherry with the object of preventing the French boats from landing, and also of obtaining provisions. In this he was unsuccessful. He then determined on proceeding to Gúdalúr (Cuddalore), which place he reached, after having been greatly harassed by Haidar's troops, who hovered about him, without affording any chance of a general action. Here he was compelled to remain inactive for four months, owing to lack of supplies. He next marched to attack the fortified pagoda of Chilambram (Chedambram) near Porto Novo, but was repulsed by the brave resistance of the garrison, whose numbers were much greater than he was led to expect. A few days afterwards the English fleet, under Sir Edward Hughes, arrived from Madras, when preparations were made for a joint attack on Chilambram. But Haidar, who had heard of the previous siege, made a forced march of a hundred miles in two days and a half, and with his whole army took up a strong position between the British troops and Gúdalúr.

On July 1, Coote, having abandoned the siege and embarked his munitions of war, advanced to encounter the enemy, hoping to dislodge them from the ground they had taken up, and to force on a general action. Forming his troops into column, with a strong baggage-guard between his right and the sea, he moved on rapidly, keeping to the east of a ridge of sandhills which intervened between him and Haidar's force. His first line at length reached an opening in the ridge, which he penetrated, after clearing it of the party that held it, and deployed again in order of battle with his front to the west. He then awaited, under a heavy fire, the arrival of his second line, which, notwithstanding repeated assaults of Haidar's cavalry aided by guns, steadily advanced and occupied a prominent sandhill near the Pass. Haidar, enraged at the gallant resistance offered by Coote's second line, directed a desperate charge of all his cavalry on both the lines of the little English force. This attack was bravely repelled, and the loss inflicted by the grape of the defenders was so heavy that Haidar was induced to withdraw, first his guns, and then all his troops, while Coote, when his two lines were united, moved on and took up a position at Mútipáliam, near Porto Novo. Haidar left the scene of battle with great reluctance, and was indeed nearly captured. He is said to have lost 10,000 men in killed and wounded. The British loss was trifling[1].

This success enabled Coote to effect a junction with a force then on its way from Bengal by the Pulicat Lake, while his onward move compelled Tipú to raise the siege of Wándiwásh, which he had invested. Thus reinforced, Coote captured the fortress of Tirupasúr, before Haidar could reach the place to relieve it, and having procured a small supply of rice, he marched to encounter that chief on the very ground which had witnessed in the previous year the disaster that befell Colonel Baillie. To Haidar that disaster seemed a prognostic of victory. On August 27, Coote's advanced guard reached the spot, and finding the enemy in force in front of them, orders were given to occupy a small thick grove on an eminence, surrounded by a water-course. The first line of his troops was promptly drawn up to confront the main body of the enemy, the second line being directed to support it, as well as the detachment holding the grove referred to. The enemy, however, poured in a heavy fire against this position, while the village of Pollilúr was occupied by them in strength, and the heavy jungle and water-courses which intervened prevented any combined action. After long delay, a brigade of our first line succeeded in seizing the village and in turning

[1] Haidar's army on this occasion is said to have consisted of 620 Europeans, 1,100 Topassis or half-castes, 40,000 cavalry, 18,400 infantry, with forty-seven guns, besides immense numbers of irregulars, and levies of various tributary chiefs.

the enemy's left. A similar movement of our second line forced their right, and enabled the English troops to gain a rising ground from which they brought their guns to bear on their opponents, and compelled them to retreat. The losses on either side were not great, nor was any material advantage gained by either of the combatants.

Coote, despairing of obtaining any decisive success, proceeded to Mádras, with the object of resigning his command, but was induced by Lord Macartney, the Governor, to resume it for the purpose of relieving Vellore[1], which was hemmed in by Haidar's army, then encamped near Sholingarh. He accordingly rejoined the British force, and after capturing Polúr on the way, proceeded to reconnoitre Haidar's position. Vellore was in the last straits, its siege having been vigorously prosecuted under the skilful supervision of French engineers, and, owing to failing supplies, its surrender was imminent. Haidar was not prepared however for an immediate attack, as he had sent out his cattle to graze at a distance from his camp, and was acting merely on the defensive. When apprised of the rapid advance of Coote's force, he at once recalled the cattle and their drivers, and getting his guns into position, opened a heavy cannonade on the

[1] The Vellore fort is of irregular shape, with massive granite walls, the upper parapets being lined with brickwork with embrasures at certain intervals. The main rampart had round towers and rectangular projections, while beneath was a fausse-braye and a broad ditch. There is a famous temple inside, called the Kaliáni Mantapam, adorned with splendid sculptures and a delicately carved roof.

leading English brigades. His guns, however, were ill served, and although his cavalry made determined charges on the first line of the English, they were met with a severe cross-fire, which thinned his ranks and compelled his retreat. In this, his troops suffered great loss from the fire of the rear rank of the English line, which faced about for the purpose. The second English line, after a severe struggle, in which it was at one time nearly overwhelmed by Haidar's cavalry, was also successful in repelling the enemy, and the Mysore troops were at last reluctantly obliged to relinquish the contest. The engagement cannot, however, be said to have been in any way decisive, although Haidar's loss is alleged to have exceeded 5,000 men.

In order to procure supplies for the starving garrison of Vellore, Coote made an expedition into the territories of the petty chiefs of the Chittúr district north of Vellore. But as Haidar had recently ravaged the country, owing to its defection from his cause, the relief derived from this source only amounted to provisions for six weeks, which Coote succeeded in throwing into the besieged fortress. Shortly afterwards he returned with his army to Madras. At the urgent request of the Government, instead of embarking for Bengal as he had at first intended, he remained at Fort St. George, and himself accompanied the troops which were despatched to succour the Vellore garrison. Though stricken down with illness, the veteran soldier accomplished the task, and having thrown in a store of provisions for three months, retraced his steps to Tirupasúr, notwithstanding a resolute attempt on the part of Haidar to bar his progress.

One other event of importance in this stage of the hostilities between Haidar and the English took place at this time. Lord Macartney, the recently appointed Governor of Madras, had received orders from home directing him to take active measures against the Dutch, then in arms against the English. Haidar, anxious to secure the co-operation of the Dutch, entered into a defensive treaty with the Governor of Negapatam, by which, in return for his aid, he agreed to make over to him the English district of Nágúr. This design was frustrated by Colonel Braithwaite, then commanding a field force at Tanjore, who not only drove Haidar's troops out of the town of Nágúr, but took by storm Negapatam itself. The occupation of this place led to the evacuation for the time by Haidar of the Tanjore territory, and of the minor posts held by him below the Gháts. The effect of the success however was not of long duration, for in February 1782, Tipú, at the head of a large force, in which were 400 Europeans, signally defeated Colonel Braithwaite who was taken prisoner. The engagement lasted during three days, and was decided by the gallantry of M. Lally, who led his French soldiers gallantly on, and made a desperate charge with the bayonet against the English square. The Mysore cavalry rushed in upon the broken square and destroyed the little English force.

Haidar had fully anticipated that the Nizám would carry out his undertaking to subdue the Sarkárs, that is, Masulipatam, Rájámandri, and other districts on the eastern coast. Nizám Alí, however, suffered Haidar to bear the whole brunt of the war, and never moved a man. The explanation of this is that Hastings, as soon as he discovered the intention of the Madras Government to make over Guntúr to Muhammad Alí, disavowed the transaction, and ordered the immediate restitution of the district, a measure which disarmed the hostility of the Nizám, who moreover feared that the Mughal Emperor had secretly promised to confer on Haidar the Viceroyalty of the Deccan. Nor had Hastings been less successful in detaching the Maráthás from the hostile combination. The Regent of Nágpúr, named Múdájí, had been induced to permit British troops to march through his territory, while Mahdají Sindhia, surprised by Colonel Carnac in the Gwalior territory, had consented to effect a peace between the Maráthás and the English. This convention, called the treaty of Salbái, was concluded on May 17, 1782[1]. Although little favourable to the E. I. Company, inasmuch as they sacrificed by it much territory, and promised to abandon the cause of the usurper Raghubá, it was so far nominally advantageous that it provided for the restoration by Haidar of all the conquests he had made from the English and the Nawáb of Arcot. The execution of this part of the treaty

[1] It was finally ratified after Haidar's death.

was impracticable, but it had the effect of severing the coalition between the Maráthás and Haidar, who thus stood alone against the English.

Haidar, although deserted by his native allies, unsupported by the French, and threatened by rebellion in his western possessions, was not a man to abandon himself to despair. He had not indeed achieved his main object of driving the English out of Southern India. But he had overrun large tracts of their country, occupied most of their principal forts, and fought steadily and with success against his antagonists. What he himself thought of the struggle is thus recorded by Wilks, as forming a topic of conversation with his finance minister, Púrnaiya :—

'I have committed a great error. I have purchased a draught of séndhi (an intoxicating drink) at the price of a lac of pagodas. Between me and the English there were grounds for mutual dissatisfaction, but no sufficient cause for war, and I might have made them my friends in spite of Muhammad Alí, the most treacherous of men. The defeat of many Baillies and Braithwaites will not destroy them. I can ruin their resources by land, but I cannot dry up the sea. I ought to have reflected that no man of common sense will trust a Maráthá, and that they themselves do not expect to be trusted[1]. I have been amused by idle expectations of a French force from Europe; but, supposing it to arrive and to be successful here, I must go alone against the

[1] The Maráthás, like the Afgháns, were generally distrusted in India. There is a well-known anecdote regarding the Duke of Wellington having driven the Gókhla chief in an open carriage, unattended, to the Maráthá camp. His agent expressed astonishment at this temerity, and being asked to explain, replied, 'You know, after all, we are only Maráthás.'

Maráthás, and incur the reproach of the French for distrusting them; for I dare not admit them in force into Mysore.'

Haidar, having despatched troops to re-establish his authority in Malabar, Coorg, and the adjoining district of Balam (Manjarábád), was about to leave the low country himself, when he received news of the landing at Porto Novo of the French troops whom he had long expected. Unfortunately for him, the convoys bearing this succour had on two occasions been intercepted and captured by British men-of-war, so that the number of soldiers actually landed was but small, while Haidar's own army was much reduced by the expeditions to the west coast. Several actions took place between the rival English and French fleets, without any decisive results. The French troops, after landing, occupied Gúdalúr (Cuddalore) and Permakoil, but their numbers did not exceed 1,200 Europeans, and M. de Bussy was unwilling to hazard a general action till he could arrive himself with further reinforcements. Nor was Coote desirous to risk a contest at a distance from his own resources, and on ground which the enemy occupied in force.

Hearing of the capitulation of Permakoil, however, he advanced towards Wándiwásh, whence the enemy retired towards Pondicherry. Finding, for the reasons above given, that they were not prepared immediately to encounter him, Coote determined to proceed to Árni, which from its central position was the chief depôt which Haidar still held below the Gháts for storing his supplies and ammunition. Coote calculated that a move on this place, which was slightly garrisoned, would have the effect of drawing out the enemy from their strong position at Kellinúr, near Pondicherry, and would at the same time facilitate his procuring supplies for his own force. He accordingly marched in that direction, but Haidar being advised of his advance, detached Tipú with a strong reinforcement to strengthen Árni, following himself the next day. On June 2, 1782, when Coote was about to encamp near the fort, he was attacked by Tipú and M. Lally. The latter lost a gun in the action which ensued, but Coote's hope of surprising the garrison failed. Although he advanced to attack Haidar, that chief by his rapid movements evaded all the attempts of the English commander to come to close quarters, and by an ingenious ambuscade decoyed the British mainguard into a position where they were charged by masses of the Mysore cavalry and suffered heavy loss. This was the last engagement in which Coote and Haidar encountered one another, and both of them died within a year.

In the month of August a force was despatched by the Bombay Government to invade Malabar. Colonel Humberstone, the commanding officer, having seized Calicut, advanced towards Pálghátcherri, capturing several small forts on the way. In the meanwhile Tipú, who had been ordered by his father to proceed at once to oppose the English, marched with great rapidity from the eastern provinces, and, reaching Malabar in October, endeavoured to cut off their communications with the coast. The English force retreated to Ponáni (Panniáni), forty miles south of Calicut, where, throwing up redoubts, and protected by two British men-of-war, they awaited the assault of Tipú's army, which is said to have consisted of 8,000 infantry, 10,000 cavalry, besides irregulars, including 600 Europeans among the troops. The English commander is stated to have had 800 Europeans, 1,000 Sepoys, and a contingent of 1,200 Travancore soldiers. Tipú, after a distant cannonade of some days, made a vigorous attack in four columns. One of these was headed by M. Lally, but was compelled to retreat, and cross the Panniáni river. There Tipú remained inactive for some days, when his whole army suddenly marched to the eastward, on the receipt of disastrous information from his father's camp.

The monsoon, coming on a short time after the contest at Árni, had compelled all the combatants in Coromandel to cease hostilities for a time. The English force returned to Madras, while the French retired to Cuddalore, and Haidar encamped with his troops sixteen miles north of Arcot. He had for a long time suffered from a cancer in his back, and the disease was aggravated by the fatigue incurred in his numerous campaigns. The skill of his medical advisers proved of no avail, and he died in his camp at Narsingh Ráyanapét, near Chittúr, on Dec. 7, 1782, or Hijri 1195[1].

[1] By the process called *abjad* (that is, a, b, j, d), in which every

letter has a numerical value, it is customary to record in India the decease of celebrated men by such a combination of letters as will give their name, or character, or the manner of their death, while showing at the same time the date of the occurrence. The most felicitous of these compositions which I have met with are the following, in Persian :—

'*Hamáyún az bám uftád*,' i. e. 'Hamáyún fell from the roof,' the numerical value of these letters, when added up, being Hijri 962/63, the year of his death, which was caused by a fall from his palace.

'*Jahángír az jahán raft*,' i. e. 'Jahángír left the world,' making Hijri 1036 the year of his decease.

In the case of Haidar, a very singular result was obtained, as shown below.

(Arabic letter) H	=	8
ai	=	10
da	=	4
r	=	200
(Arabic *ain*) A	=	70
l	=	30
í	=	10
(Arabic guttural) Kh	=	600
á	=	1
n	=	50
ba	=	2
h	=	5
á	=	1
du	=	4
r	=	200
Total		1195 being the Hijri year of Haidar's death.

The following verse on his tomb brings in this remarkable combination of letters :—

'Kih ín Sháh ásúdah rá chist nám?
Chih tárikh rahalat namúdah ast ú?
Yaki z'án miyán guft tárikh wa nám
Kih "Haidar Alí Khán Bahádur" bigú.'

'What is the name of this lamented sovereign?
What is the date shown of his departure (decease)?
One from among them (the bystanders) told the date and name
Say "Haidar Alí Khán Bahádur."'

CHAPTER XVI

Haidar's Character and Administration

Before narrating the circumstances which followed Haidar's demise, and the course of events during the reign of his son Tipú Sultán, it may be appropriate to refer to the character, public and private, of the distinguished soldier who from obscurity raised himself to a throne, and made his name a terror to his foes. As regards the memorable warlike operations in which he took a leading part, the accounts derived from English and French sources are so conflicting, owing to the rivalry of these nations, and their struggles for supremacy, that an absolutely impartial estimate of his military reputation is well-nigh impossible. It may safely be asserted, however, that in their dealings with the natives of India at this period the French were more sympathetic than their hereditary enemies, the English. Although the French did not, like the Portuguese, lose their nationality by too intimate social relations with the people of the country, their attitude to them was more genial and attractive than that of the English, whose national temperament, although compelling respect, and, as in the case of Clive, unbounded military devotion, did not inspire affection. It was for this reason probably that Haidar, when first mounting the ladder of his future success, was inclined to seek the support of the French; and, throughout his struggles with the English, they were found in numbers in his army, and gallantly assisting him in his various enterprises. It must be remembered, too, that the name of Dupleix was still a rallying war-cry to those who were opposed to English ascendancy, and that the issue of events was so uncertain that no one could foresee which of the two rival European powers would ultimately become the master of Southern India.

Haidar was a born soldier, an excellent rider, and skilful alike with his sword and his gun. Trained by early habits to active exertion, he could undergo great fatigue without suffering from it, and when at the head of his troops, he was reckless of personal danger, thus stimulating the courage of his followers. Cool and sagacious in war-time, he excelled in cavalry tactics, and seemed to possess by intuition the knowledge how to launch his horsemen with the greatest effect on the enemy. It may be doubted, however, whether in an open field he was able to cope with the Maráthá hordes, while, having no acquaintance with practical engineering, he had to rely in the sieges which he undertook on the ability and skill of the French officers in his service. Perhaps his most remarkable characteristic was the celerity with which he made forced marches on various occasions, always with a successful result, feats which could only have been performed by a man who was both hardy and daring. The celebrity of his name, and the rich opportunities for plunder which his numerous expeditions offered, attracted to his standard vast numbers of recruits, who, although he was niggardly in his payments, were firmly attached to him and fought gallantly under his orders. To the French who were in his service he appears to have been generally considerate, and to have placed great reliance on their fidelity and the bravery of their officers.

As regards his administrative capacity, it may be said that, owing to his being constantly engaged in war, and therefore absent from his capital, he was necessarily compelled to confide much to subordinate agents; and although his experience of Bráhmans, based on the treachery of his early ally Khande Ráo, was unfavourable on the whole, he had no option but to entrust this capable, though not always trustworthy caste, with most of the details of revenue management. Haidar's remedy for neglect of duty and for egregious plundering, to the detriment either of the peasantry or the treasury, was the scourge, which he applied freely, often perhaps justly, but always with severity. It may be said that the 'Korla,' a whip with a very long lash, reigned supreme, floggings being of daily occurrence, as related by the missionary Schwartz, and few officials appear to have escaped the infliction, which is not extraordinary when one considers that Haidar did not hesitate to apply the discipline to his own son. Nevertheless, although his training had been defective, and his policy often dictated severe punishments, it does not seem that he was wantonly brutal, or that he took a pleasure in torturing his prisoners. Sad tales might indeed be told of many of his English captives, who were half-starved, and sometimes forcibly circumcised[1]; but the manners of the time were savage, every man's hand being against his neighbour, while the English soldier was regarded by the natives as a ferocious beast who could only be subdued by main force.

He had no compunction in devastating whole tracts of his own country in order to prevent an enemy from subsisting his troops on local supplies, nor did he evince any compassion for the conquered, or show liberality to the distressed. His every action was regulated by a cold calculating temperament, but he rewarded handsomely those who served him well, and thus secured their attachment. In marked contrast to his successor, he was entirely free from bigotry,

[1] There is a curious little book, published in 1824, which relates the captivity of one James Scurry, who, having been taken prisoner by the French, was, with several others, handed over by the French admiral Suffrein at Gúdalúr to Haidar, by whose orders the party, which comprised fifteen youths, was sent to Seringapatam, where, having been previously drugged, they were all circumcised. His statement is confirmed by James Bristow, an artilleryman, who, when a prisoner, was compelled to undergo the same rite. This individual, after an imprisonment of nearly ten years, escaped from the hill fort of Hutridrúg, suffering terrible privations till he reached an English camp near Kopal. He speaks in terms of gratitude of the kindness of some Mysore women who supplied him with food on his perilous journey. He published a narrative in 1794.

being indeed wholly indifferent to religious sentiments, and he cared not one jot what faith his officials followed, so long as they obeyed his behests.

In person he is described as of medium height with rather coarse features, which were embrowned by the sun; his nose small but aquiline, his eyes also small, and the lower lip thick. Contrary to the custom of most Orientals, and especially of Musalmáns, he had neither beard nor whiskers. Although not addicted to wearing jewellery, he was not devoid of vanity in dress, the body and sleeves of his habit fitting neatly, and being drawn close by strings, while the rest of his robe was ample and hung in folds. His turban was of brilliant scarlet, flat at the top, and of immense length. When with the army, he wore a uniform of white satin with gold flowers, faced with yellow, drawers of the same material, and boots of yellow velvet, with a scarf of white silk round his waist.

He is said to have been very accessible to all and to have conversed with great readiness. In close intercourse with his boon-companions he did not hesitate to make use of the foulest abuse. In matters of business his shrewdness and capacity were remarkable, and he had the faculty of giving his attention to several subjects at the same time, so that he could hear a letter read, dictate orders, and witness a theatrical exhibition all at once, without being distracted by any one of these occupations. Although he was unable to read or write, the answer to every document of importance was read over to him by a second person after it had been written by one of his scribes, thus ensuring absolute accuracy, after which he scrawled his signature[1]. All State business was transacted under his own eyes with regularity and despatch, his retentive memory enabling him to supervise closely everything that was done by his subordinates. The evenings were enlivened by comedies, and the performances of trained groups of dancing girls, and not unfrequently ended in a debauch with some chosen friends. He had an extensive harem, and did not scruple to seize and place in it any girl who possessed superior attractions; but he never allowed his sensuality to incapacitate him from attention to his public duties, while great allowances must be made for him, considering the time in which he lived, and the license which results from protracted warfare.

On great occasions he made a magnificent show with his chosen troops. His regiments of cavalry, in which were many Europeans, headed his procession; then followed 500 warriors mounted on camels; after which came the state elephants with richly embroidered trappings; then two regiments of Abyssinian horse, wearing plumes of red and black ostrich

[1] The writer possesses a Maráthá grant issued by him, in which the signature is simply the Arabic letter 'h' for Haidar, twice repeated, in an inverted form, thus ђђ for ح. Very few Indian princes at this time wrote their names at the end of their communications, the official seal at the head of such documents being confirmed by an impression of the signet-ring, which was rarely taken off the chief's finger.

feathers, and carrying steel-headed lances; followed by infantry wearing large silk scarves with drawers reaching to the thigh, and armed with lances to which small bells were attached. Next came the nobility, gorgeously arrayed, covered with chain-armour, and splendidly mounted. Then came the Nawáb's own horses, richly decorated, and led by grooms. To these succeeded a troop of running footmen, and then the principal officers of the household, with chains of gold hanging down their breasts. Lastly, at the end of the procession came Haidar himself, mounted on a white elephant[1] which was captured in the Bednúr country. The rear consisted of a large number of elephants, five of which carried special royal insignia[2], and after them two more regiments of Abyssinian cavalry, and a crowd of foot-soldiers of the same nation, who closed the procession. On each side of the line of march moved a body of infantry clothed in white silk with long black lances, plated with silver, and adorned with small red streamers at the tips. The whole made up a gallant array, which could only be surpassed by that of the Great Mughal himself.

Haidar certainly failed in accomplishing the object

[1] The so-called white elephants, which were so highly esteemed by the sovereigns of Burma and Siam, were not really white, but of a dirty red-brick colour, as was probably that of Haidar.

[2] The first carried a mosque of gold; the second the 'Máhi marátib,' or the fish-emblem, usually granted by the Mughals; the third a flambeau of white wax in a gold casing; the fourth two golden pots, called *chambú*; and the fifth a round chair, inlaid with ivory, and covered with gold.

he had in view at the close of his long and stormy career. But his want of success was mainly due to the duplicity of his native allies, and to the supineness of the French Government, which reserved all its strength for its operations against us in North America, and seemed quite indifferent to recovering the prestige it had lost in India. Had it despatched a sufficient army to the Coromandel coast when Haidar was operating against the Madras forces, there can be little doubt that Fort St. George would have fallen, and that the British authority would have been supplanted by the French flag. De Bussy arrived too late, and with Haidar's death, and the success of Hastings' diplomacy, commenced the final decline of French influence in India.

Whatever defects may be justly attributed to Haidar as a ruler, or in his private life, he was a bold, an original, and an enterprising commander, skilful in tactics and fertile in resources, full of energy, and never desponding in defeat. For an Oriental he was singularly faithful to his engagements, and straightforward in his policy towards the British. Notwithstanding the severity of his internal rule, and the terror which he inspired, his name is always mentioned in Mysore with respect, if not with admiration. While the cruelties which he sometimes practised are forgotten, his prowess and success have an abiding place in the memory of the people.

TIPÚ SULTÁN

TIPÚ SULTÁN

CHAPTER I

Tipú's Accession to the Throne

Tipú Sultán, on the death of his father, now assumed the sovereignty of Mysore. Born in 1753 at Devanhalli, the place where Haidar first distinguished himself, he was named after a Musalmán devotee at Arcot, for whom Haidar had a special veneration. His mother, Fakhr-un-Nissa, was a daughter of Mír Moín-ud-dín, for some years Governor of Kadapa. When the time of her delivery was nigh, it is said that she paid a visit to the shrine of the holy man, to obtain a blessing, and gave her child the name which he afterwards bore [1].

[1] There has been much discussion both as to the etymology and the meaning of the word Tipú. In the inscription on his tomb the name is written Típú, and it is often so pronounced in Mysore, but on his seal it is unmistakably Tipú, which mode of spelling the name has been adopted in this sketch. As regards the meaning of the word, although it has been asserted that Tipú is the Kanarese for a tiger, this is certainly erroneous. Independently of the improbability of a holy man, such as Tipú Mastán Áuliah, after whom Tipú was named, being called by the designation of a

When it became apparent that Haidar's end was approaching, his ministers, Púrnaiya and Krishna Ráo, took every precaution to conceal the gravity of his malady from the army. Immediately after his death, express messengers on fleet camels were despatched to apprise Tipú of the event, and to urge his return with all speed, while Haidar's body, having been embalmed, was forwarded privately to Kolár in a coffin resembling a chest containing valuable spoil. Matters were so well arranged that the secret of his demise was kept for many days, not only from the English, but from his own army, only the most trusty officers being made acquainted with the occurrence. The troops marched westward, Haidar's closed palankeen being carried with the army as if containing an invalid. If any suspicion were aroused by his not showing himself, no open demonstration of incredulity took place.

Meanwhile Tipú, who received intelligence of his father's death in the short space of four days, broke up his camp near Panniáni, and proceeded by forced marches towards the main army, which had halted on the Pennár river awaiting his arrival and the junction of French troops. His appearance in the camp was hailed with joy, and he at once assumed the control of affairs, having at his disposal

ferocious beast, the word for a tiger in Kanarese is 'huli.' How the mistake arose is shown at the end of this sketch. Tipú Mastán Áuliah's tomb at Arcot bears the date 1142 Hijri, or 1729 A.D., and was erected by Nawáb Saádat Ullah Khán, who died in 1732.

at least 90,000 troops, and a vast treasure hoarded at Seringapatam.

Had the Madras Government at this juncture adopted energetic measures, it is probable that the defeat of the Mysore army would have ensued. But the veteran Sir Eyre Coote had been compelled by ill health to resign his command, and the Madras authorities, though aware of Haidar's death and of the difficulty which had arisen owing to the want of a leader for his troops, allowed a month to elapse before they ordered a force to the front to engage the enemy.

CHAPTER II

Capture of Bednúr by General Matthews—Its Recovery by Tipú

When the Bombay Government heard that Colonel Humberstone was threatened in Malabar by Tipú's army, they despatched General Matthews with a small force to relieve him from his precarious position, and to effect a diversion by seizing the territory held by Mysore on the coast. This expedition had accomplished with success the reduction of Rájámandrúg and Honáwar[1] in North Kánara, taking also several of Haidar's ships, when intelligence of that chief's death induced the Bombay authorities to send peremptory orders to General Matthews to seize Bednúr. Having embarked his small force, Matthews landed at Kundápur, and in three days reached the foot of the Hosan-

[1] About twenty miles from Honáwar are the celebrated Gersoppa Falls, on the River Sharavati, which, though of less volume than those of Niagara, form a sublime spectacle. The Rájá Fall (one of four) leaps down a sheer depth of 830 feet into the abyss below, being met halfway down by the Roarer Fall, another tremendous cataract. The whole scenery is of extraordinary beauty. The depth of the great fall was carefully plumbed in 1856 by two officers of the Indian navy, who contrived to sling a cradle across the top of the abyss, and launching themselves in it, let down a line to the bottom.

gadi Pass. The ascent from this to Haidargarh at the top of the *ghát*, a distance of about eight miles, is tremendously steep, rough, and stony. Great boulders obstruct progress, with here and there a piece of slippery pavement in the worst parts of the defile. One gigantic rock is called the 'Áné Jerí,' from a tradition that an elephant was thence precipitated over the precipice. Modern skill has made this and several others of the old Mysore passes practicable for carts. At the time referred to, although thousands of bullocks yearly traversed it, the natural difficulties were so great, that had it been resolutely defended, Matthews could not possibly have reached the summit. But Colonel Macleod, who had joined him from Panniáni, had in his small detachment His Majesty's 42nd regiment, to whom from early associations hills and rocks were doubtless no serious obstacle. These gallant men, followed by the native troops, carried at the point of the bayonet one breastwork after another with little loss, although some of the batteries were armed with numerous guns, and defended by thousands of the enemy.

Bednúr fortress was at this time governed by Shekh Ayáz or Haiyát Sáhib, a Náir of Malabar, who had been forcibly converted to Islám, and for whom Haidar had an extraordinary affection on account of his fidelity and trustworthiness. Tipú, however, resenting this partiality, had a personal dislike to him, and had sent orders to supersede him in his post. But before his successor, Lutf Alí Bég, could reach his destination, Ayáz, distrusting his sovereign's intentions towards him, and despairing of holding his own against the English, surrendered the fort and town of Haidarnagar to Matthews.

It is not clear what advantage the Bombay Government expected to gain by the temporary occupation of a district so far removed from any support, and in the heart of an inaccessible country. To Tipú it was of supreme importance to recover possession of it before reinforcements could be forwarded to the English general. He accordingly assembled a considerable army, and, dividing his troops into two columns, despatched one of them to cut off all communication with the coast, and with the other invested the town of Haidarnagar. In the meantime, Shekh Ayáz had fled with an immense treasure, and succeeded in making his way to Bombay. The English troops, being only 1,600 in number, of whom 400 were Europeans, were totally insufficient to defend the extensive fortifications, erected at different places in the heavy jungles which surrounded the town. Indeed Tipú experienced little difficulty in forcing the positions they held, and compelling the garrison in the fort to surrender. He had the mortification, however, to find the treasury empty. So irritated was he at this unexpected result that, although Matthews had capitulated on condition that his troops should be permitted to withdraw unmolested to the coast, the conqueror placed him, with many other officers and men, in irons, and sent the party to Seringapatam, where it is said Matthews was constrained by starvation to eat poisoned food, of which he died[1]. It was asserted that Tipú was partly urged to commit this breach of faith owing to a detachment of Matthews' force having cruelly put to death the inhabitants of Anantpur, an outlying town in the Bednúr territory. But Wilks, who had ample means of ascertaining the real facts, declares in his history that the allegation was entirely devoid of truth.

[1] Some accounts say that he was despatched with the butt-ends of his guards' matchlocks.

CHAPTER III

SIEGE OF MANGALORE—TIPÚ'S CRUELTIES

MANGALORE, the principal seaport in South Kánara, had been captured once by an English fleet, but was recovered by Haidar in 1768. It again surrendered, however, to General Matthews, prior to his attack on Bednúr, the commandant declaring the post to be untenable. Tipú, determined to regain possession of the place, despatched a small force to seize it, but the attack was frustrated. He then resolved to besiege it in person with the whole of his army. Although he gained at the outset some slight advantages by driving in the outposts, and thereby causing a temporary panic in the ranks of the British troops, Colonel Campbell, the commanding officer, resolutely held the fort, which was ill adapted for defence, in spite of the vigorous attacks made upon it by the Mysore troops, aided by the skill of French engineers. Tipú's heavy guns, however, had nearly reduced the fortifications to ruins, and an assault was daily expected, when news was received of the cessation of hostilities between the English and French. The officers of the latter nation who were in the Mysore service honourably declined to act any longer against the English, notwithstanding every inducement to them on Tipú's part to continue the siege. They accordingly withdrew from the scene of operations; and Tipú, indignant at the repulses he had met with in his attacks on a place which was avowedly weak, converted the siege into a blockade. The garrison, being short of provisions, were reduced to the greatest distress, but still held out bravely. Tipú agreed to a temporary armistice, to the terms of which, however, he did not adhere, his object being to starve out the defenders. The instructions of the English admiral forbad the captain commanding the squadron to resort to any hostile measures during the period prescribed by the preliminary articles of peace between the two European nations. The result of this inaction was that the defenders of Mangalore were so insufficiently supplied with food, that disease broke out, and the hospitals were filled. On a council of war being held, it was resolved to surrender, the brave garrison being permitted to retire to Tellicherri, 80 miles to the south, according to the terms of a treaty which was executed in January, 1784. By this convention Tipú recovered possession of all the territory held by his father in Kánara and Malabar. Before returning to the upper country, he signalized his zeal for the faith of Islám by driving out of the coast region no fewer than 30,000 of its Christian inhabitants, who were forcibly deported into Mysore. His own account of this infamous transaction is that the Portuguese, having on pretence of trade obtained settlements on the western coast, had prohibited Musalmáns from practising their faith, and expelled Hindus from their territory, those who remained, in spite of the prohibition, being enrolled as Christians. He added that, in process of time, they won over the local Rájás to tolerate their proceedings, and by cajoling the pliant population, made numerous converts to their 'abandoned religion.' 'His Majesty, the shadow of God,' so runs his bombastic effusion, 'being informed of these circumstances, the rage of Islám began to boil in his breast. He ordered that an enumeration and description of the houses of all Christians should be made, and then sent detachments under trusty officers who, after early prayers, acting in accordance with their instructions, seized 60,000 (*sic*) persons, great and small of both sexes, who were carried to the resplendent presence. They were then despatched to the capital, and the males being formed into battalions of five hundred each, under the command of officers well instructed in the faith, were honoured with the distinction of Islám, and distributed in the principal garrisons.' These unfortunate people received the appellation of 'Ahmadi' or 'praiseworthy,' and the date of their forcible conversion was commemorated by the phrase, 'God is the protector of the religion of Ahmad [1].'

[1] It is stated that Tipú demanded the surrender of the daughters of some of these Christians in order to have them placed in his seraglio, and that, on the refusal of the parents, the latter had their

Similar cruelties were practised on the people of Coorg, the small hill district where Haidar had barbarously cut off the heads of all who opposed his progress. Some resistance having been made to the Mysore Governor, Tipú marched into the country with his army, and lectured the Coorgs on the iniquity of their custom of polyandry. He warned them that if any further rebellion took place he would extinguish it by removing the population and Islámizing them. At a later period he actually carried this barbarous threat into execution, devastating the province, and driving the wretched inhabitants like sheep to Seringapatam, where they had to submit to circumcision and the sanctifying rites prescribed by the despot.

noses, ears, and upper lips cut off, and were then paraded through the streets on asses, with their faces towards the tails of the animals.

CHAPTER IV

Colonel Fullarton's Military Operations

Just before the death of Haidar, Mr. Sullivan, the English Resident at Tanjore, an official of exceptional ability, had devised a scheme for co-operating with Colonel Humberstone in Malabar, by sending an expedition to Pálghát, *viâ* Coimbatore. But this plan, being opposed, or at any rate unsupported by Sir Eyre Coote, had fallen through. Mr. Sullivan now sought to forward the views of his Government by entering into negotiations with one Tirumal Ráo, who professed to be an emissary of the Mysore Ráni, with the object of restoring to power the imprisoned Rájá. This design being approved by the British authorities, a force was despatched under Colonel Lang, which occupied various places in the Coimbatore and Madura districts. Colonel Fullarton shortly afterwards succeeded to the command. On learning that Admiral Suffrein was about to disembark French troops at Gúdalúr, he marched in haste to that place, but on his arrival heard of the cessation of hostilities between the European powers.

Being apprised however of Tipú's violation of the

armistice at Mangalore, Colonel Fullarton moved at once on Pálghát from Dindigal to relieve the distressed garrison. He was encouraged in this effort by reports of disaffection among the Mysore troops, and of a widespread conspiracy to overthrow the usurper. But the latter combination, though it actually existed, was, fortunately for Tipú, detected, and all the leaders in it were summarily executed[1], except two who were placed in iron cages. Fullarton, notwithstanding many natural obstacles, due to heavy rain, and the vast forest which skirts the Anamalai Hills, succeeded in forcing his way to Pálghát, which surrendered to his arms. Then finding it impossible to advance at once to Tellicherri on the coast, he proceeded to Coimbatore, which he captured. Before however he could make any further progress, he received an intimation that negotiators were being sent to Tipú to arrange terms of peace, and he was directed to abstain from further hostilities.

As his force consisted of 13,000 men, and as he himself was an officer of great ability and energy, it is probable that his junction with the British troops on the west coast would have led to a complete defeat of Tipú. But, as we have seen on previous occasions, the vigorous efforts of the English military commanders were paralyzed by the timidity and hesitation of the civil authorities at Madras. European diplomatists, with rare exceptions, are no match for the duplicity and craft of Orientals.

[1] Some were blown from a gun, and others impaled.

It is not therefore surprising that, after protracted negotiations, in which the Madras envoys were subjected to much humiliation, Tipú signed in March, 1784, a peace for the mutual restitution of the places which the two powers had seized, and for the surrender of all prisoners, a convention by which he sacrificed little, and was able to boast that the English had cringed before him. The natural result was that he re-occupied all the southern part of Malabar, and that the fruits of Fullarton's enterprise were thrown away. Even as regards the hundreds of persons languishing in prison, and the thousands whom Tipú had forcibly carried away from their homes, he studiously evaded surrendering more than a very limited number. Indeed, the great majority of those who had suffered imprisonment had either perished from the hardships they endured, or had met with a violent death at the hands of Tipú's executioners. Many of the English officers, besides General Matthews, had been ruthlessly murdered, by poison or other foul means, while natives of the country had been frequently sent to die at Kabáldrúg.

CHAPTER V

CAMPAIGN AGAINST THE MARÁTHÁS

TIPÚ'S next military operations were conducted against certain chiefs in the country between the Krishna and the Tungábhadra. These chiefs, having succumbed to Haidar, had evaded paying the tribute due to him, knowing well that they would be supported in their contumacy by the Maráthás, to which nation most of them belonged. The principal malcontent was the Deshái or Jágírdár of the strong hill fort of Nargúnd[1], who, with his cousin of Rámdrúg, a neighbouring fort, relied upon aid from Poona, and refused to submit to Tipú. The Mysore army besieged both places, the latter falling speedily, notwithstanding Parasu Rám Bháo's attempts to relieve it. Venkat Ráo, the chief of Nargúnd, valiantly defended that town for some months, but was at last compelled to capitulate.

[1] In 1858 Bháskar Ráo, the Jágírdár of this State, murdered Mr. C. Manson, the political agent in the southern Maráthá country, and for this crime was hanged, the territory being confiscated, but the Rámdrúg portion of it had been previously severed from it.

The promise of personal safety given to him was however set at naught, and on his surrender he was sent in chains to die miserably at Kabáldrúg.

This expedition, though professedly undertaken for the purpose of strengthening his weak northern frontier, implied extraordinary self-sufficiency and arrogance on the part of Tipú. He should have known that by provoking a collision with the warlike hosts of the Maráthás, guided by the astute policy of Náná Farnavís and containing such leaders as Mahdají Sindhia and Tukojí Holkar, he would bring down upon himself a cloud of enemies. Moreover, the peace with the English was but a hollow truce, and the Governor-General had shown a tendency to seek an alliance both with the Maráthás and the Nizám. In the beginning of 1786 the two latter powers, having arranged all the preliminary conditions, despatched their conjoint forces to invade Mysore, the Maráthás being commanded by Hari Panth, and the Nizám's contingent by Túhavvar Jang. Tipú, who had just returned from Coorg, advanced to encounter them, having first assumed the title of King (Pádsháh). After ordering his general, Búrhán-ud-dín, to stay the advance of the allies, who had captured Bádámi near Nargúnd, he himself proceeded to besiege Adoni, then held by the Nizám's troops. Muhabbat Jang, nephew of the Nizám, having vainly striven to buy off Tipú, owing to the town being the residence of many ladies of his uncle's and his own family, defended it so gallantly, that Tipú, notwithstanding repeated assaults, was compelled to abandon the siege. As the rainy season was approaching, the Nizám's youngest brother, Mughal Alí Khán, by feigning to attack the Mysore troops, succeeded in concentrating their attention upon himself, thus permitting of the evacuation of the place and the escape of the ladies across the Tungábhadra, before the river filled. When Tipú returned to resume the siege, he found the town deserted, and had to content himself with razing the fortifications.

He now commenced a series of operations which evince much skill and enterprise on his part. Having seized a small fort which commanded the passage of the Tungábhadra, Tipú, in spite of the opinions of his chief officers, succeeded in crossing his army over the swollen river. He then marched along the left bank in order to effect a junction with Búrhán-ud-dín, which he accomplished without much difficulty, and proceeded to meet the enemy in the vicinity of Sávanúr. After many desultory engagements, which led to no result, he at last dislodged them from their position, and captured the town, the Nawáb having previously fled to the Maráthá camp. The siege of several minor forts was then successfully undertaken, when Tipú, early in 1787, expressed his readiness to make peace, agreeing to pay at once thirty lacs of rupees on account of tribute due, and a further sum afterwards. Adoni, Nargúnd, and other strongholds were surrendered by him to the Maráthás. The pacific overtures made by him on this occasion, when he had obtained many successes over a formidable foe, can only be explained by his anticipation of renewed hostilities with the English.

CHAPTER VI

Tipú's Reforms in Malabar—Embassies to Europe

On returning to Seringapatam, Tipú directed the entire destruction of the old town of Mysore, in order to obliterate all associations with the deposed Rájás. He next proceeded to Calicut, which offered him a fine field for showing his zeal for Islám by reforming the pestilential customs of the province. He at once issued a proclamation, denouncing the practice of polyandry [1], and informing the people that if they did not desist from such a pernicious usage, they would all be 'honoured with Islám,' and

[1] The existence of this custom is referred to by Camoens in the Lusiad thus:—

> 'Géraes saõ as mulheres; mas somente
> Para os da géracaõ de seus maridos:
> Ditosa condiçaõ, ditosa gente,
> Que naõ saõ de ciumes offendidos!'
>
> (Verse 41, Canto VII.)
>
> 'Son commune le donne in frá coloro
> Che son de la progenie de' mariti:
> Felice condition del viver loro
> Che de la gelosia non son feriti.'
>
> (Italian version.)

The custom appears to have prevailed also in Coorg.

their headmen deported to Seringapatam. With this object he appointed sundry religious teachers to supervise their domestic morals and teach the true faith. Local officers were also nominated to collect the revenue. Having, as he imagined, put the people in the right path, and ensured their welfare in this world and in that to come, he marched to Coimbatore and Dindigal, wasting the territories of such minor chiefs as had withheld their allegiance. He returned in triumph to his capital, where he occupied himself in reforming his troops, dividing them into brigades, according to their several tribes, sayyads in one battalion and shekhs in another. On leaving Malabar, he had made over the government to Mír Ibráhím, who, by his exactions and disregard of all written engagements, precipitated a rebellion of so serious a nature that Tipú, though surprised at the ill-success of his own benevolent measures, was compelled to proceed in person to suppress the revolt.

Marching through Coorg with a large army, he sent detachments about the country to hunt down the rebellious Náirs, while he himself proceeded to Kútipúram. Here, two thousand of their race defended themselves and their families with resolution, but were soon obliged to surrender. This gave an opportunity to Tipú to show his apostolic zeal. Orders were issued that the whole of these unfortunates should be offered the alternative of becoming good Musalmáns, or, in case of non-compliance, that they should be banished to Seringapatam. They reluctantly acquiesced in the former alternative, knowing well what the deportation meant. The next day, accordingly, all the males were circumcised, while both sexes were compelled to eat beef, as a proof of their conversion. One of the principal victims of Tipú's revenge was the Rájá of Chirakkal[1], of ancient descent, who, having been falsely accused of conspiring, was attacked and killed, and his body hung up after his death. In this raid the Mysore sovereign is said to have carried off large treasures plundered from the temples in Malabar. He crowned his achievements by compelling the princess of Cannanore to marry her daughter to his son, Abd-ul-Khálik.

On the conclusion of the treaty with the Madras Government at Mangalore in 1784, Tipú, inflated with notions of his own prowess, and inspired with hostile feelings against the English, was most anxious to unite himself closely with the French, by whose assistance he hoped to subvert the power he both feared and hated. With this object he sent an embassy, which was instructed, after sounding the views of the Sublime Porte, to repair to France to secure the co-operation of that Government. But the reception which his envoys met with at Constantinople, where Tipú's name had probably never been heard of, was so unfavourable, that they returned in a rage. In 1787 a second embassy, headed by

[1] It is from the descendants of this house that females are adopted into the royal family of Travancore.

Muhammad Darvesh Khán, was despatched direct to Paris, where the delegates were received most graciously by Louis XVI and hospitably entertained. Louis was himself, however, environed by domestic difficulties, and the cataclysm which shortly afterwards overwhelmed his country was rapidly approaching. He therefore contented himself with profuse promises of future support, and the ambassadors returned to India, discredited, to meet the wrath of their master.

CHAPTER VII

Invasion of Travancore

It will be remembered that in 1766 Haidar Alí overran Malabar. Among the chiefs who then tendered their submission was the Rájá of Cochin, whose territory abutted on that of the Travancore Rájá. In 1761 the Zamorin of Calicut had invaded Cochin. The Rájá had sought aid from his neighbour who despatched a force under General de Lanoy, which drove out the Zamorin, and the reward for this service was the cession of a tract of country on which fortifications were erected, extending thirty miles from an estuary on the coast to a range of inaccessible hills. A strong fort was built at Kariapilli on the coast, while a wall 20 feet thick and 12 feet high, with stone batteries and bastions at intervals, was constructed all along the frontier. It was further protected by a deep ditch, while bamboos and thorny shrubs were planted close to the wall on the side of the ditch. These defences were called the 'Travancore Lines,' and were intended to resist attacks from Malabar. Haidar, after his invasion of Malabar, had coveted Travancore, but the opposition of the Dutch at Kranganúr (Kadangúlúr), and his own military operations on the eastern coast, arrested his designs.

Tipú was aware that the possession of Malabar would give him command of the western coast, thus facilitating the importation of munitions of war, and enabling him to attack the English from two sides. He therefore determined on its conquest. It was not difficult for him to find plausible pretexts for the attack which he meditated, partly on the ground that the Travancore Rájá had erected the defences on the territory of his feudatory the Cochin chief, aggravating the insult by purchasing from the Dutch the forts of Kranganúr and Ayakota, and partly by reason of Travancore having afforded protection to rebellious fugitives from Malabar. He at first endeavoured to secure the aid of the Cochin Rájá in his designs. But that chief evaded his demands, and Tipú proceeded to attack the defences, regardless alike of the remonstrances of Travancore and the objections of the Madras Government, to which the latter State owed allegiance.

On December 28, 1789, Tipú's army, under his personal command, appeared before the walls, his force consisting of 14,000 infantry and 500 pioneers. By daybreak of the 29th, his troops had gained an entrance and taken possession of a part of the ramparts to the right, the Travancore soldiers contesting each post, but being compelled to retreat before the enemy till they were forced back upon a strong position where, with the aid of a small gun, they made a stand. Fresh troops were ordered up by Tipú to carry the building, and support the leading corps. But the movement was clumsily performed, and in the confusion which ensued, a small body of the defenders, who were posted in a thick cover close to the ramparts, threw in such a heavy fire that the assailants were repulsed, and a panic ensued[1]. The whole of Tipú's army was soon in precipitate flight, he himself being carried away by the rush. The ditch was filled with the bodies of those who were forced on from behind and trampled under foot before they could extricate themselves. The bearers of Tipú's palankeen were among the fallen, and he himself escaped with the greatest difficulty, through the exertions of some faithful servants, but lamed in the efforts he had made to save himself. In the hurly-burly he lost his sword and shield, which were taken away in triumph to Trivandrum, the capital of Travancore. He is said to have lost no less than 2,000 men in this miserable affair.

Lord Cornwallis, then Governor-General, had intimated to the Madras Government his readiness to consider impartially any claim which Tipú Sultán might urge against the sale to the Travancore Rájá

[1] The Sultán's panegyrist, Mír Hussén Alí Khán, ascribes this disaster to the Travancore troops having broken down a mound which had been erected to prevent the inroads of the sea, its destruction causing the tide to rush in, and prevent any support being given to the leading detachment.

of the places above referred to. At the same time he pointed out the inadvisability of submission to untenable demands. When he learned that Tipú had by his rash action shown his contempt for any pacific overtures, he despatched on March 30, 1790, explicit instructions to the Madras Government not to allow a faithful ally to be overwhelmed by an insolent and cruel enemy.

Tipú had, indeed, forwarded to Madras a lame explanation of his attack upon the Lines, alleging that his troops were merely searching for fugitives, and had accidentally come into collision with the Travancore army. But he had no intention of desisting from his purpose, and, smarting under the defeat which he had sustained, he ordered siege-guns to be despatched at once from Seringapatam, and recommenced the attack. Batteries were erected close to the defences in the early part of March. Yet although Tipú spoke with derision of the 'contemptible wall,' nearly a month elapsed before the ramparts were destroyed. A breach being then effected, the Travancore troops were compelled to retreat, and Tipú directed the immediate demolition of the fortifications, sending off as spoil to his capital 200 pieces of cannon, and a vast quantity of ammunition.

At the time when the assault of the Lines took place, there were two English regiments of native troops at Ayakota, belonging to the Madras establishment, as well as one European regiment, and two of

Sepoys, which had been despatched from Bombay to the same place. But the vacillation of the Madras Government, and want of enterprise on the part of the commanding officers themselves, prevented their co-operating with the Travancore troops in the defence.

The Mysore army, flushed with success, now began to lay waste the country with fire and sword, desecrating and despoiling temples, and burning towns and villages, whose wretched inhabitants fled to the hills, where many were seized and made prisoners. The ruins to be seen at the present day testify to the ferocity of the invaders, while all the records of antiquity and the archives of the Travancore State were consumed in the burning pagodas, public offices, and houses. These atrocities were perpetrated with the express sanction of Tipú Sultán, who himself marched with his main army southward to Alwái, a favourite watering-place of the Travancore Rájá. He contemplated the reduction of the whole province. The Díwán, Kasava Pillai, had, however, strengthened the garrisons at the principal posts, and constructed stockades along all the backwater-passages on the coast, so as to intercept the progress of the enemy. In the meanwhile the monsoon set in, and the whole country was soon under water, so that no communication could be maintained except by boats. Tipú, despairing of accomplishing his purpose under these adverse circumstances, and hearing that the English were assembling an army at Trichinopoli, was compelled to withdraw his troops in haste and retreat to Pálghát, losing a large number of men on his way. The local chronicler grandiloquently compares his abrupt departure with the disastrous retreat of Napoleon from Moscow.

CHAPTER VIII

Lord Cornwallis declares War—Want of Success of General Medows—Siege of Bangalore—Attack upon Seringapatam

Tipú's aggressions, and his wilful disregard of treaties, had now become so reckless that the Governor-General had no option but to declare war. Lord Cornwallis, who then held the supreme power, was a man of stern rectitude, an experienced soldier, and not disposed to allow the British Government to be trampled in the dust. For some time he had foreseen that hostilities were inevitable, and that the half-measures of the Madras authorities had only increased the pride and presumption of the Mysore potentate. So far, however, he had contented himself with warnings and remonstrances, but the unprovoked attack of Tipú on the Travancore State decided him to take active steps to put a stop to further aggressions on allies of the British. When information reached him of the assault on the Travancore Lines in December, 1789, he entered into a treaty of offensive and defensive alliance with the Maráthás and the Nizám for the purpose of curbing

Tipú in his hostile proceedings, and exacting reparation. He had, indeed, proposed to conduct personally the operations which he deemed necessary, but learning that General Medows had been appointed Governor of Madras, he was content to leave to that experienced officer the prosecution of the impending war. When Tipú was apprised of the preparations being made to oppose him, he imagined that he might cajole the new Governor as he had done his predecessor, and wrote accordingly, suggesting that matters might be amicably settled by envoys on both sides, and asking for a safe-conduct for his own ambassador, but was met with the stern reply that an attack upon an ally of the English was tantamount to a declaration of war upon themselves. The Mysore ruler, accustomed to the procrastination and hesitation which he had previously encountered at the hands of the Madras authorities, took this reply as being significant, and immediately left Coimbatore for Seringapatam to make preparations for defending his territory.

It may be questioned whether the plan of operations conceived by General Medows was not of greater magnitude than was practicable with the means at his disposal. His army was so distributed that the main portion under his own command should reduce the whole of Coimbatore from Karúr, on the Trichinopoli frontier, westward to Pálghát, and then ascending the Gajalhátti Pass, should enter Mysore above the Gháts, while a separate force under

Colonel Kelly was to invade the Báramahâls to the eastward. No special difficulty was met with in occupying the several posts in the Coimbatore district, while both Dindigal and Pálghát fell with little resistance on the part of the garrisons. But when a division under Colonel Floyd had established themselves at Satyamangalam on the north side of the river Bhawáni, twenty miles east of the Gajalhátti Pass, Tipú, leaving his heavy baggage at the top of the *ghát*, descended the pass with a large body of cavalry, supported by many guns, and attacked the British force. Part of his army crossed the river by a ford, and some detachments in coracles or basket-boats, while the remainder operated from the northern bank, with orders to seize Satyamangalam. The attacks of the Mysore troops were gallantly resisted by the small British force, both sides losing heavily; but it became evident that it was impossible to hold Satyamangalam, and Colonel Floyd was unwillingly compelled to retreat. He was hotly pursued by Tipú, who kept up a heavy fire with his guns.

The British troops having halted, a sharp action ensued. On a report being spread that General Medows had arrived, the Sultán, despairing of success, drew off his army. Floyd's detachment arrived safely at Velládi, where General Medows met them, having returned from Dhannáyakankóta on the way to Gajalhátti. Tipú, imagining that the General's march was a manœuvre to get between him and Seringapatam, retired across the Bhawáni, while the British troops returned to Coimbatore. They were there joined by Colonel Stuart's division, which had captured Pálghát. The main object of this enterprise —that is, the invasion of Mysore by the Gajalhátti Pass—had, however, been successfully frustrated by Tipú. Relieved of any immediate apprehension about his capital, he now marched rapidly southwards, taking Erode, Dhárápuram, and other places; then hearing of the invasion of the Báramahál district, he proceeded thither with the greater part of his army. During this inroad, the British troops in vain pursued him, being baffled by the rapidity of his movements, while his cavalry, always hovering about, gave him precise information whenever the British marched, and at the same time intercepted and seized all persons sent out by the English general to obtain intelligence.

While General Medows was attempting to carry out his project of forcing the Gajalhátti Pass, his second *corps d'armée*, amounting to 9,500 men and partly composed of native troops sent from Bengal, proceeded, in accordance with instructions, to reduce the Báramaháls. It was commanded by Colonel Maxwell, Colonel Kelly having died before active operations were commenced. On November 1 Maxwell reconnoitred the stronghold of Krishnagiri, the capital of the district. Distrusting his ability to besiege it with success, he retired on Káveripatam, but his intention of surprising Krishnagiri was foiled by the rapid movements of Tipú. The latter, anticipating the approach of Medows, attacked Maxwell with his cavalry, and strove to bring on a general action before the junction of the two English armies. This design, however, was frustrated owing to the strong position occupied by Maxwell. He remained strictly on the defensive, in expectation of the arrival of Medows, who, crossing the Káveri at Erode, reached the Thopúr Pass on the 14th, and effected a junction with the other army on November 17. Tipú, however, was too skilful a general to be caught in a snare, which would have compelled him either to fight or to retreat up the Gháts, so he determined to double back by the Thopúr Pass, from either end of which the British force was more than twenty miles distant, and to lay waste the country on the south.

This movement he carried out, although he ran the risk of being cut off by the English force, which marched on the same day for the pass. Fortune favoured him through the inertness of Medows who forbad Colonel Stuart, commanding the right wing, from attempting to attack a large body of the Mysore infantry while in the defile, an operation which that officer was confident of accomplishing with success. The progress of the English army was so slow and cautious that Tipú's troops were able to clear the pass with little loss, leaving however their baggage and camp equipage on the other side. Emerging into the more open country, the Sultán directed his march towards Trichinopoli, but finding the Coleroon river so swollen that to cross it would be impracticable, he changed his course. He proceeded due north through the heart of the Coromandel country, burning and destroying all the villages on the road, and exacting heavy contributions from the people. The English general, who had followed in pursuit, was so ignorant of his movements that he supposed him to have crossed the Coleroon and gone southwards. About the middle of December, the Mysore army invested the fort of Tiágarh, but was repulsed after a short siege. Tipú next advanced to reduce Trinomalai and Permakoil, both of which places surrendered to his arms. He then marched to Pondicherry in the expectation of receiving a promise of support from the French authorities; but the Governor, while engaging to make known his proposals to his own Government, was unable to hold out any immediate guarantee of assistance. Tipú stipulated for the aid of 6,000 men, all expenses of transport and clothing to be paid by him, and engaged with this help to destroy the English altogether in India, and to give France possession of their territory. The King of France, when Tipú's offer was made known to him, although conscious of the advantages of the proposal, was reluctantly compelled to discourage it, not being indeed himself in a position to guarantee any material aid.

The Mysore sovereign may be said in this campaign to have shown greater skill in strategy than the English general who was opposed to him. But destiny had declared against him on the western coast, where his commanding officer, Hussén Alí, was signally defeated by Colonel Hartley; while the Governor of Bombay, General Abercromby, landing at Tellicherri, reduced Cannanore, so that by the end of 1790 the whole of Malabar was freed from Tipú's sway. It must be admitted, however, that by his energy and the celerity of his movements Tipú had for a time checked and discomfited his opponents, who, instead of occupying any part of his territory, found themselves attacked in the very centre of their own possessions.

At the end of January, 1791, Lord Cornwallis, the Governor-General, who had arrived at Madras in the previous month, assumed personally the command of the army then assembled at Vellore, and determined to undertake the siege of Bangalore. Tipú, on hearing of his advance towards the Mysore country, hastened to prevent his ascending the Gháts from the Báramahál. But Lord Cornwallis, by a feigned march on Ambúr in that district, took the main army first north, and then due east, to the Múgli Pass, which he reached in four days without opposition. The ascent was found to be comparatively easy, and in a few more days he was joined by his siege-train. When his equipments were perfected, he marched towards Bangalore by way of Kolár and Hosakote, both of which places made no resistance, and encamped fifteen miles from the object of attack. Tipú endeavoured to harass his movements by his cavalry and rocket-men, and next day drew up his troops as if to seek an engagement. Thereupon Lord Cornwallis sent the rear of his army to confront the enemy, and gave orders for the heavy guns and the rest of his force to pass to the right behind this cover and proceed direct to Bangalore. They arrived there the same evening (March 5), followed by the portion of his army which had faced Tipú's troops.

The fortress of Bangalore, constructed in the sixteenth century by Kempe Gáuda (the Red Chief), was originally of mud, but in 1761 it was, by order of Haidar, enlarged and strongly rebuilt in stone. It was of oval shape, with round towers, five cavaliers, a fausse-braye, and a deep ditch. The glacis, however, was defective, and the flanking defence imperfect. To the north of it was the pettah or town, also encircled by a deep ditch and a thick-set hedge of thorns [1], which had sufficiently protected the place against the Maráthá horse. It has now a population of 180,000 including the cantonment, and even at the time mentioned was a commercial town of importance; indeed the second in rank in the Mysore kingdom.

The day after his arrival Lord Cornwallis moved his force to a stronger position. Tipú Sultán was about to encamp to the south-west of the fort, when the English cavalry, which had been sent out to reconnoitre, fell in with a division of his troops which

[1] This hedge was entirely removed about 1861, and the ditch filled up and levelled.

they attacked, but were routed with loss after a sharp contest. On March 7, Lord Cornwallis issued instructions for assaulting the town. This was a task of great difficulty, the impenetrable thicket concealing the actual state of the defences, while the gate which was the point of attack was built up behind with strong masonry, and for a long time baffled the troops, upon whom a severe fire was directed from the turrets. Heavy guns were then brought up, and the gate was at last forced, but not without considerable loss. Among the fallen was Colonel Moorehouse in command of the artillery. The Sultán made a desperate effort to recover the town, sending a large force with positive orders to regain possession of it, but after a prolonged contest his troops were repulsed on all sides, and obliged to evacuate it.

During the ensuing siege of the fort, Tipú Sultán for some days contented himself with cannonading the English troops, apparently having in view the destruction of the park of artillery which contained the siege ammunition. On the 20th, foreseeing the probability of an early assault, he massed his army on the heights to the south-west, to protect some heavy guns that he had brought up to enfilade from an old embankment the works of the enemy, which were now advanced nearly to the top of the glacis. Lord Cornwallis, perceiving the danger that threatened his approaches, moved out his troops as if to attack the Mysore army. This had the effect of making the Sultán order the withdrawal of the guns in question in order to support the position he held. They were brought back again, however, in the evening, which induced the English commander to make immediate arrangements for an assault the same night, a breach having been effected in the curtain to the left of the gateway. At eleven o'clock the ladders were planted to ascend the fausse-braye and a projecting work on the right. The garrison sounded the alarm, and a desperate struggle took place on the breach; the commandant of the fort, Bahádur Khán, heading an obstinate resistance when the British troops gained the ramparts. The assailants, however, overcame all opposition, charging with the bayonet. Then filing off to right and left by alternate companies, they met over the Mysore gate, and descended into the fortress before any help from outside could reach the garrison. The enemy had despatched two separate columns to attack the British, but in both cases they were driven back with great slaughter. The advance of a third body of his troops along the sortie by the Mysore gate was checked by a few shots from the guns on the ramparts now held by the assailants. The carnage had been great, and upwards of one thousand bodies of Tipú's troops were buried, while the casualties in the British army during the whole siege amounted to about five hundred.

Although Tipú had expected that an assault would be made, and had moved his army at nightfall to within a mile and a half of the Mysore gate of the fortress, in order to support its defenders, he was unprepared for so immediate and disastrous a result. The first intimation which he received of the success of the enterprise was the arrival in his camp of the disheartened garrison who had evacuated the place. Finding that all was lost, his next thought was to provide for the defence of his capital. Meanwhile Lord Cornwallis, after making the necessary repairs of the Bangalore fortress, marched in about a week's time to Devanhalli, with the object of effecting a junction with a body of 10,000 cavalry despatched by the Nizám. This he accomplished after long delay, caused by imperfect information, and the British army, accompanied by the undisciplined and heterogeneous host of their ally, marched towards Seringapatam, taking the southern route by Kánkánhalli[1], through a wild but picturesque country. Thence they proceeded to Arikere, about nine miles east of Seringapatam, which they reached on May 13, without meeting any opposition. Tipú, in contravention of the engagements he entered into at Mangalore in 1784, had retained in captivity no fewer than one hundred English, men and boys, most of whom had perished through ill-usage. About nineteen of the youths, who had been trained to dance and sing, still survived, and were now cruelly put to death, lest their detention should be brought to light[2]. The

[1] The fateful rock of Kabáldrúg, so often mentioned, is only a few miles west of this place.

[2] It has never been explained why these unfortunate people were allowed by the Madras Government to languish in captivity after the signing of the treaty of 1784.

despot took care also to remove from the walls of the houses of Seringapatam the caricatures of the English, with which his artists had ornamented them.

Lord Cornwallis, on approaching Seringapatam, found the Mysore troops drawn up in a strong position, with the Káveri on their right, a rugged hill on their left, and a swamp in front. Seeing the improbability of attacking them with success on this ground, the English General resolved to attempt by a night march to turn their left flank by crossing the heights some distance to the right, but a heavy storm coming on defeated this design. The next morning he determined if possible to bring on a general action from the hill which his troops had occupied. They proceeded to descend the ravines to a rocky ridge intervening between the two armies. Tipú then promptly changed his front, and succeeded in first getting possession of this ridge, whence a heavy fire was poured on the advancing English column, while bodies of cavalry endeavoured to break their line. An attack upon the ridge by the battalions under Colonel Maxwell was however successful, and the Mysore infantry retreated down the opposite descent, after losing some guns in the struggle. The remainder of the English army then advanced to attack the main body of the enemy, who were gradually driven, after a fierce resistance, from height to height. The English cavalry under Colonel Floyd charged the rear of their retreating infantry, inflicting heavy loss.

The success would have been complete had it not been for the accidental or intentional bungling at this juncture of the Nizám's cavalry. This enabled the Mysore troops to escape nearly unscathed, with almost all their guns, some of which they had before hurriedly abandoned. The pursuit was, after a short interval, resumed; but the enemy had meanwhile withdrawn under the cover of the guns to the island of Seringapatam. The victory, although a splendid one, was not decisive or final. The English army was sorely crippled from the want of supplies both for men and cattle, so many of the latter having succumbed from lack of fodder, that most of the heavy guns had to be dragged by the troops. To add to Lord Cornwallis' perplexity, the enemy's light horse had effectually intercepted all communications, and he had received no intelligence of a column of British troops which had been ordered to join him from the western coast.

This second British force had in fact entered Mysore from Coorg by the Heggala Pass, and proceeded as far as Periyápatam, thirty-five miles from Seringapatam. But Lord Cornwallis, finding it impossible to move his heavy guns, sent orders to Sir Robert Abercromby, who commanded the division, to return forthwith to Malabar. These instructions were carried out, most of the cattle died on the way, and it was found necessary in consequence to bury the battering-train at the summit of the pass into Coorg. The Mysore cavalry keenly pursued the retiring force, plundering the baggage and killing several men, while our gunpowder, having been deposited in a temple, was set fire to. The explosion destroyed the temple itself and a great part of the town. Lord Cornwallis, finding his position no longer tenable, and all communication cut off, destroyed his siege-train, threw his shot into the river, and burning his carts and tumbrels, retired on May 26 towards Bangalore. Tipú Sultán, who had thus again escaped the fate which was impending over him, fired a royal salute from his ramparts and illuminated his capital. Cornwallis' troops were half-starved, and suffered greatly on their return eastward from the inclemency of the rainy season. On approaching Chinkurâli (Cherkúli) he was fortunately met by two Maráthá armies, of whose approach Tipú's skirmishers had kept him in ignorance, and his immediate necessities were thus relieved.

CHAPTER IX

Military Operations of the Maráthás and the Nizám

A passing reference may here be made to the measures taken by the Poona Darbár and the Nizám, whose co-operation the Governor-General had secured, to prosecute hostilities against the Mysore ruler. The principal gain which the Maráthás hoped to secure from the alliance was the recovery of the territory between the Krishna and the Tungábhadra which Raghubá had made over to Haidar as the price of his support. An army of 10,000 horse and 10,000 foot was placed under the command of Parasu Rám Bháo, one of the Patwardhan Bráhmans, who, aided by a small reinforcement of British troops from Bombay, proceeded to besiege Dhárwár, the capital of the province, September, 1790.

Dhárwár was then held by Badar-uz-zamán, who had under him about 10,000 men, regular and irregular. He resisted all attacks for three months, and although an escalade was attended at first with some success, it ultimately failed owing to the Maráthás beginning to pillage and burn the town. The conflagration enabled the commandant to drive them out in the confusion. In the beginning of January, 1791, fresh British troops arrived, without guns or stores. The next month preparations were made for an assault, but just as the assailants were about to advance from their cover, the commandant lodged lighted portfires among the fascines which filled the ditch, and blew up the causeway. The enterprise thus failed, and although Parasu Rám Bháo soon afterwards received some heavy guns from Poona, and mining operations were again prosecuted, little real progress was made. It was not till March 30 that the brave commandant, owing to scarcity of provisions, surrendered the fort which he had held for six months. The fall of Dhárwár led to the speedy reoccupation by the Maráthás of the whole province. Parasu Rám Bháo crossed the Tungábhadra and marched towards Seringapatam, while another force under Hari Panth proceeded by a more easterly route by way of Sírá in the same direction. The two armies effected a junction with Lord Cornwallis' troops at Cherkúli, as mentioned at the end of the last chapter.

Nizám Alí's contingent, aided by a small British force, assembled near Haidarábád in May, 1790, and, after protracted delays, invested the stronghold of Kópal[1]. The fort held out until April, 1791, a period

[1] This fortress is twenty miles west of the ruins at Hampi (the capital of the old Vijayanagar dynasty), which are of great interest to the archaeologist. The vast temple of Vittala is supported by richly carved monoliths twenty feet high, immense granite slabs forming the roof.

of five months, when intelligence of the capture of Bangalore in the previous month induced the garrison to surrender. The Nizám's troops then marched to the south-east, to regain possession of the Kadapa territory and the adjoining districts. A large force of his cavalry also proceeded to join Lord Cornwallis' army, on its way to Seringapatam.

Tipú had, on various occasions since the British army entered Mysore, written evasive letters to Lord Cornwallis, expressing a desire for amicable negotiations, and complaining of the conduct of the Travancore Rájá. These overtures for a reconciliation were repeated the day after the Governor-General broke up his camp near Seringapatam, and a short time afterwards he sent a Bráhman to make advances to Lord Cornwallis. But the envoy, having been prohibited from negotiating with any one except the Chiefs of the allies, declined to treat with deputies, and returned to his master without effecting any result.

CHAPTER X

Capture of Nandidrúg—Disaster at Coimbatore —Storming of Sávandrúg—First Siege of Seringapatam

Lord Cornwallis, having returned to Bangalore, arranged with the Maráthás, to whom he made a loan of fourteen lacs of rupees, that they should proceed to Sírá to operate in the north-west, while the Nizám's forces were entrusted with the duty of occupying the territory to the north-east. He himself marched to the Báramahâls to reduce the forts in that district, and to keep open the communications with Madras.

All the forts, except Krishnagiri, capitulated or were seized, but there were still some strongholds occupied by the Mysore troops which intervened between him and the Nizám's army. The chief of these was Nandidrúg, a stupendous rock-fortress, 4,800 feet above sea-level, and thirty miles north of Bangalore, the natural strength of which had been increased by the chiefs of the adjoining town of Chikballapur. On the summit is an extensive plateau, in the centre of which is a deep hollow, with a wood and a fine reservoir containing an abundance of water.

The fortifications were extensive, and the descent on all sides but one was precipitous. The south-west angle formed a tremendous cliff, now called 'Tipú's Drop,' from a tradition that prisoners were hurled over it by orders of the Sultán. An extremely steep and almost impracticable path leads down direct to the town beneath, but this was quite inaccessible to troops, and the only side on which an approach could be made was strengthened by a double line of ramparts. A spirited defence was made by Lutf Alí Bég, the commandant, the garrison using their guns with effect, and rolling down huge masses of rock on the assailants. But notwithstanding the difficulty of dragging guns up the rugged hill to play on the walls, and the want of cover, two breaches were made after an interval of three weeks. On October 19 an assault was ordered, and the fort was carried in the most gallant manner, after a sharp struggle, and with little loss. The splendid rock is now, owing to its salubrious climate, a favourite resort of the Europeans at Bangalore.

These successes were to some extent counterbalanced by the failure of Colonel Maxwell to seize Krishnagiri, while an unexpected reverse befell a small detachment which occupied Coimbatore. Tipú Sultán, having heard of its weak state, sent a considerable force to invest Coimbatore, but it was energetically defended by Lieutenant Chalmers and a young Frenchman named De la Combe. With a small body of half-caste Europeans and some Travancore soldiers, though furnished only with small guns and bad ammunition, our garrison repulsed all the attacks of the Mysore troops. Scarcely however had the slender defences been repaired, and some guns captured from the enemy been mounted on the walls, when Tipú's General, Kamar-ud-dín, came in sight with a force of 8,000 regular infantry, a body of horse, and eighteen guns and mortars. Meanwhile a detachment under Major Cuppage was approaching to relieve the garrison, leaving at Pálghát a large number of cattle destined to equip General Abercromby's army. Kamar-ud-dín made a dash for the pass which, however, Cuppage after a severe action retained possession of, but was compelled to return to Pálghát. Kamar-ud-dín then resumed the siege of Coimbatore with vigour, and, after a stout resistance, compelled the defenders to surrender. Although on capitulating, Lieutenant Chalmers and his companion Lieutenant Nash, who had brought him some slight assistance from Madura, were assured of a safe-conduct to Pálghát, Tipú refused to ratify the stipulation, and after a detention of several days they were sent as prisoners to Seringapatam.

Lord Cornwallis, having now made all his arrangements for prosecuting the siege of the Mysore capital, proceeded first to reduce several formidable hill-fortresses, the continued possession of which by the enemy might interrupt his communications. The chief of these was Sávandrúg, a stupendous rock of granite, 4,000 feet above sea-level, and resembling in appearance a gigantic whale. There are two peaks on the summit, one called the black, and the other the white peak, separated by a chasm, and both supplied with plenty of water. The mountain is smooth and precipitous on all sides, with a circumference of many miles, and was surrounded by a thick jungle of bamboos and other trees which made the rock unapproachable. Even at the present time the ascent is difficult, the granite boulders and grass being very slippery. The bluff bold sides of the rock are very imposing, and from the summit there is a splendid view commanding the approaches on every side. To reduce such an inaccessible stronghold seemed an impossibility, and Tipú certainly deemed it to be unassailable; yet the feat was performed in an incredibly short space of time, and with hardly any casualties.

Part of his troops being so disposed as to prevent any relief coming from the west, Lord Cornwallis entrusted to Colonel Stuart the task of cutting a road for the guns through the heavy jungle to the foot of the rock. When this difficult work had been achieved and the heavy ordnance had been got into position, the batteries on December 17 opened on the lower wall of the defences, 1,500 feet above the base. In three days a breach was made in this wall, but above this again was another wall erected on a precipitous height, and occupied in strength by the garrison. On a sufficient elevation for the guns being attained, this latter wall was found to be of slight construction, and the next morning it was speedily demolished, and an immediate assault ordered. The precipitous face of the rock was soon covered by the storming party, who, heedless of the dangerous nature of the ascent, succeeded in gaining the citadel on the eastern peak, the defenders being so taken by surprise as to offer no opposition. Meanwhile, another division, after climbing the rock above the breach, made its way towards the western peak, whence the commandant of that citadel had sallied to attack the assailants of the eastern peak. Met midway by our second division, and seeing that shots from the batteries below were falling among his men, he retreated to his post, but was so closely followed that pursuers and pursued entered the citadel together, the commandant falling at its gate. This notable feat of arms was followed by the capture by escalade of the fort of Hutridrúg (Utradrúg), and the reduction of several other minor strongholds, all of which, except the first, were seized without much resistance.

The toils were now being closely woven round the 'tiger,' and Lord Cornwallis commenced his march on Seringapatam. He encamped six miles to the northward of that capital on February 5, 1792, having been joined by the main army of the Nizám, which was accompanied by Sir John Kennaway the Resident at Haidarábád. The remainder of Nizám Alí's troops had been detained in the ineffectual blockade of Gurramkondá in the Kadapa territory, while the Maráthá hosts under Parasu Rám Bháo were engaged in the congenial occupation of plundering the northern and eastern part of Mysore. Only a small portion of their troops under Hari Panth marched with the British army.

Seringapatam, or Srírangapatan, is a place of considerable antiquity, and is situated at the western end of an island three miles long and one wide. It derives much of its celebrity from two temples built there about a thousand years ago (894) by one Tirumalaiya [1]. In the time of the Vijayanagar dynasty, about 1454, a fort was erected on the island by Timmanna, to whom had been confided the government of the Ashtagráma, or eight townships on either side of the Káveri, which constituted the district. The stones for this fortress were obtained by the destruction of numerous Jáin temples in the vicinity. From the time of its seizure by Ráj Wodiar in 1609, successive Rájás had given attention to the defences, and they had been further added to by Haidar and Tipú. The river, full of rocks and frequently unfordable, was in itself a serious obstacle; while along its banks, huge walls with lofty cavaliers and deep ditches cut through solid granite increased the natural strength of the position. On the northern face were strong redoubts, supported by an inner fort. Beyond all and outside the island was an almost impassable belt of thorny trees extending from the river, first due north and then in a south-easterly

[1] A peculiar sanctity is attached by Hindus to a point in the Káveri called the 'Paschima Váhan,' or 'western flow,' where the river, making a sudden turn, flows to the west instead of to the east, contrary to the regular course of the stream.

direction to the Karigat hill, where it again encountered the Káveri. The number of guns on the northern defences is said to have been three hundred, while the garrison inside and outside the fort comprised 45,000 infantry and 5,000 cavalry.

Lord Cornwallis, without consulting his allies or waiting for the co-operation of General Abercromby who had been ordered to advance from Malabar, determined to attack this formidable position the day after his arrival. Accordingly, dividing his troops into three columns at night, he not only forced the Sultán to withdraw from his advanced posts, but succeeded in establishing himself on the eastern part of the island, after securing possession of the ford over the river. This was not accomplished without severe fighting, every point being obstinately contested, and the enemy returning repeatedly to the attack, from which they did not desist till daylight. Tipú had taken up his post in a redoubt which bore his name, but finding that his centre had been penetrated, and that the enemy were making for the ford, he retired into the fortress. In the confusion that ensued, vast numbers of the Coorgs, who had been made to serve compulsorily in his army, contrived to escape to their own country. On February 7, 1792, the Sultán made a desperate effort to retake the redoubt, sending his choicest troops, including the French in his service, to attack it. All his attempts were repulsed, nor was an endeavour to dislodge the British from the island more successful.

Preparations were now made for assaulting the fort itself. Meanwhile General Abercromby's force had advanced from Coorg, and joined the main army on February 16. The frightful atrocities committed by the Sultán in the beautiful hill province of Coorg had left an indelible impression upon the people, and although Víra Ráj, the ruling Wodiar or chief, was too weak to resist the vast army of Mysore, he had on many occasions ravaged the part of the country which lay on his borders. The Coorg headmen held their land on a military tenure, all the able-bodied men of their several families being bound to serve their chief in his military expeditions. Although undisciplined, they made a gallant array in their blue surtouts and red sashes, with their long carbines, and the national broad-bladed wood-knife, called Kádkatti, which they wore on the back.

Víra Ráj had been imprisoned in Mysore for six years, and only effected his escape at the end of 1788. Remembering his own vicissitudes, and the terrible disasters which had befallen his country, he was eager to avail himself of the friendship proffered by the British Government when hostilities with Mysore were impending. With this view he readily entered into an alliance with our agents in 1790, binding himself to treat Tipú as an enemy, and to furnish all possible supplies, while the E. I. Company on their part guaranteed his independence. This convention, as will be seen presently, gave immense umbrage to Tipú, who was well aware of the value of the Coorg province from a strategical point of view.

The Sultán was greatly enraged on seeing that the English army had deliberately cut down, for the purpose of making fascines, the cypresses and other trees in the Lál Bágh, where his father's tomb had been erected; and it must be admitted that this act of vandalism was, though perhaps unavoidable, one that might well rouse his wrath. He vented his rage by firing his guns at the garden, and every other post occupied by the enemy, but seeing the active operations of the British army for the prosecution of the siege, he began to consider seriously the consequences to himself and his capital.

The opportune arrival of the Bombay army, consisting of 2,000 Europeans and 4,000 Sepoys, enabled Lord Cornwallis to arrange for attacking Seringapatam on both sides of the Káveri, and on Feb. 19, General Abercromby took up a position on the south-west of the river. The movement was sharply contested by the Sultán's troops, who were, however, driven back, though they repeated the attack on the 22nd, with a like result.

During the progress of these operations, Tipú had thought it advisable to sound the views of Lord Cornwallis by despatching envoys to his camp, in order to arrange the terms of a convention, and on the 22nd received an intimation of the preliminary conditions which the allies offered for his acceptance. They specified the cession of half his dominions, the payment of over three millions of rupees, the release of all prisoners, and the delivery of two of his sons, named Moíz-ud-dín and Abd-ul-Khálik, as hostages. Tipú, after consulting his principal officers, assented to the general tenor of these terms, and duly signed the contents of the document submitted to him, remitting shortly afterwards a million of rupees in part payment of the sum stipulated. But when he found that the province of Coorg was mentioned in the detailed list of the territory which was to be severed from his control, his rage knew no bounds. For a long time he refused to sign the final treaty, and it was only when he saw indications of the siege being recommenced, and was told that the negotiations would be broken off, unless he at once accepted the proffered terms, that he at last gave way.

In estimating Lord Cornwallis' policy, it must be remembered that soldiers are ordinarily more generous than other negotiators to a conquered foe, and that he deprecated a further conflict which would entail a great sacrifice of life. Moreover, he was probably fettered by restrictions placed upon him by the E. I. Company, who, while unwittingly founding an empire, were still walking in commercial leading-strings. Tipú was undoubtedly an usurper, as his father had been before him; the lawful Mysore Rájá, though a captive, was still alive; and Tipú had not hesitated to avow himself the implacable enemy of the English. The Sultán was hemmed in on all sidės, and Seringapatam must inevitably have fallen had the siege been prosecuted. It must be confessed, moreover, that it was a dubious policy to restore to power a bitter foe, thus enabling him to resume a hostile attitude which eventually compelled Lord Mornington to crush for ever the despot's arrogance[1].

Cornwallis was of opinion that he had effectually curbed Tipú's power of disturbing the peace of India, a mistaken idea, of which subsequent events showed the fallacy. The restoration of the lawful Mysore dynasty does not appear to have been contemplated, nor would the captive Rájá have been able to main-

[1] It was about this time that the Sultán gave his sanction to the publication of certain encomiastic effusions about himself, which are sufficient evidence of his vanity. The following are extracts from one of these productions :—

'When the Rustam-hearted King rushed forward on the charger of his anger, then did the hearts of the English lions quake with fear.

'The flash of his sabre struck the army of Baillie like lightning: it caused Munro to shed tears, resembling the drops from the clouds.

'On Lang's heart was fixed a stain, like that of the tulip: Coote was made by this calamity to lament.

'When the Maráthás behold the army of our King, the dread thereof causes them to flee like deer.

'The Firingi (European) and Nizám-ul-Múlk pass night and day together, trembling with fear of our King.

'The Hajjám's (meaning 'barber' in derision for Nizám) army flees through dread of thee, as the hunter does when he beholds the lion.

'Compared with him Hátim was a miser; Socrates, Hippocrates, and all the sages of the earth appear before him like ignorant children; Mars dwindles before the valour of our King to a mere infant.

'Owing to the justice of this King, the deer of the forest make their pillow of the lion and the tiger, and their mattress of the leopard and panther.'

tain his rule unsupported by British troops. The territory held by his predecessors at the time of Haidar Alí's usurpation formed but a portion of the Mysore dominions in 1792. These considerations were probably factors in inducing Lord Cornwallis to refrain from the extreme measure of dethroning Tipú Sultán.

As soon as Tipú had recovered from the humiliation to which he had been exposed, his first step was to order contributions from all his subjects. Even the soldiers were not exempted from this forced levy, which was applied to the purpose of liquidating his debt. It must be admitted that, so far as the English Government were concerned, he faithfully discharged his obligations. The hostage princes, Abd-ul-Khálik and Moíz-ud-dín, who had been in charge of Major Doveton, were in consequence returned to their father in 1794. But the burden which was imposed upon the cultivators, from whom three times the amount required was exacted, was disastrous in the extreme and greatly impoverished the country. Assiduous attention was paid to strengthening the fortifications of Seringapatam, and the Sultán then proceeded to introduce various changes and so-called improvements in his administration, of which an account will be given further on.

CHAPTER XI

Tipú's Secret Machinations

In 1793 Lord Cornwallis left India. He was succeeded by Sir John Shore, afterwards Lord Teignmouth, who, although possessing a profound and extensive acquaintance with all questions relating to revenue administration, had not the political capacity which was needed to keep in check so aggressive and self-sufficient a character as Tipú. In 1796, the Mysore Rájá, Chámráj, died, leaving an infant son, to whom Tipú did not think it expedient to give even the titular status of Rájá. It became apparent about this time that although the tiger's claws had been clipped, he had not been deprived of the power to do mischief. There was a stipulation in the Seringapatam treaty that if Tipú should molest either of the contracting parties, the others should unite to punish him. But in 1795 he entered into a covert engagement with Alí Jáh, son of the Nizám, then in rebellion against his father, to assist him on condition that, in case he succeeded in dethroning the Nizám, he should make over to Tipú Sultán all the territory lying south of the Tungábhadra and Krishna rivers then held by the Nizám. This scheme was, however, foiled by the prompt action of M. Raymond, commanding a body of French troops in the Nizám's service. Alí Jáh was taken prisoner.

Tipú next deputed an embassy in 1796 to the court of Zamán Sháh, the Afghán ruler, seeking his aid as a co-religionist, and making magnificent promises of co-operation, with a view to the subjugation of the Maráthás and the expulsion of the English from India. Nor did he confine himself to these overtures. He also used every means in his power to foment misunderstandings between the Peshwá, Sindhia, and the Nizám on the one hand, and the English on the other, so as to sever the connexion of the native chiefs with the British. The previous attempts of the Sultán to bring about a close alliance between the French and himself had hitherto proved abortive; but now that open war had broken out between the two great European states, which had so long been rivals in India, the time seemed to him propitious for renewing negotiations. Among the curious papers found subsequently in the palace of Seringapatam is a document relating the proceedings taken by a body of French citizens in the pay of 'citizen Tipú.' Fired by enthusiasm for the recently constituted French Republic, the Frenchmen assembled to the number of fifty-nine at Seringapatam, and elected as their president citizen Francis Ripaud, who is styled a Lieutenant in the French navy. After passing several resolutions testifying their devotion to the republic and their hatred of royalty, they hoisted on May 14, 1797, the national flag. They next repaired to the parade in the city, where they were received by the Prince (the Sultán), who, after firing a salute of 2,300 (*sic*) pieces of cannon, assured them of his affection and support. To this they replied by declarations of unfailing devotion to his cause. Amidst a profound silence, the tree of Liberty was planted, surmounted by the cap of Equality. Ripaud then made a speech in which the following passage occurs:—

'Je vois le comble de la barbarie et celui de l'atrocité—Dieu! j'en frémis d'horreur! Quoi! Je vois ces victimes de la férocité anglaise qui ont été sciés entre deux planches! des femmes victimes de leur brutalité et assassinées au même moment. Oh! comble d'horreurs! mes cheveux se redressent! Que vois-je? Des enfants encore à la mamelle, je les vois teints au sang de leurs mères infortunées. Je vois ces malheureux enfants expirer de la même mort que leurs malheureuses mères. Oh! comble d'horreur et de scélératesse, que d'indignation tu inspires! Soyez persuadées, âmes infortunées, que nous vous vengerons. Oh! perfides et cruels Anglais, tremblez! Il est un Dieu, vengeur du crime, qui nous inspire de laver dans ton sang les atrocités que tu as commises envers nos pères et leurs malheureuses compagnes. Apaisez-vous, âmes plaintives de l'innocence, nous jurons de vous venger. Oui, je le jure!'

These ardent Jacobins seem to have inspired Tipú, not only with an idea of their 'hault courage,' as Kingsley would say, but also of their ability to be of material service to him. Although Monsieur F. Ripaud was in all probability a scamp of the first water, and his pretensions were ridiculed by the Sultán's officers, that sovereign, who in his own eyes was wiser than all his court, determined to purchase his vessel and send ambassadors in it to the Isle of France (Mauritius), to solicit from the Governor the aid of a fleet and an army. From a note in Tipú's own handwriting it appears that he was singularly ignorant both of geography and history. The following are entries in this document, which professes to be a catalogue raisonné of the heads of departments of the French administration:—

'Names of the three islands belonging to the English—Ireland, Guernsey, Jersey.' 'On the English island there was once the Rájá of a tribe called Coosea (Ecosse ?)—a hundred years ago, the English Rájá put the Rájá of the Cooseas to death, and took possession of his country.'

On April 2, 1797, Tipú addressed a letter to the authorities (Sardárs) of Mauritius, professing his attachment to the French, and dwelling upon the friendship which had long subsisted between them and the Mysore State from the time of his father, Haidar Alí. 'The shameless, thieving, robbing English, of themselves incompetent,' had, he said, leagued with the Maráthás and the Mughal (Nizám), and forcing him to make peace, had extorted from the 'God-given State' three crores and thirty lacs of rupees, besides wresting from him half his finest provinces. He therefore sought aid from the French to expel the iniquitous English from Hindustán, asking them to furnish both Europeans and Negro troops to assist his own in this desirable object. Ripaud's deputy, who was to have sailed with the envoys, decamped however in a boat with the purchase-money of the ship just before their embarkation, and the embassy was consequently delayed; nor did it leave till October, when Ripaud himself, by Tipú's desire, accompanied it. The ambassadors reached the Isle of France in January, 1798, when the absurdity of Tipú's proposals became apparent. He asked for 10,000 French troops, and 30,000 Habshis (Negroes), who, he asserted, with the co-operation of 60,000 men on his part, would be enabled to subdue both the Maráthás and the Nizám, reduce Madras to ashes, and expel the English entirely from India. He even entered into minute details as to how that result was to be accomplished; but the envoys were not provided with funds, though they were profuse in promises. General Malartic, the Governor of the Isle of France, saw that Tipú had been gulled by Ripaud. He nevertheless received the ambassadors in state, and promised to at once transmit their master's requisition to France. Knowing, however, that he could himself render no assistance, he contented himself with issuing a proclamation calling for volunteers. The result was that about one hundred French subjects accompanied Tipú's envoys on their return to India, landing at Mangalore in April, 1798 [1].

[1] The reports which the envoys submitted to Tipú on their return are curious and interesting, but too long for quotation.

They relate their ill-treatment by Ripaud when at sea, their sufferings from mal-de-mer, the surprise which their arrival at Port Louis caused to the French authorities, and the civility shown to them by these officials. They show clearly enough that Ripaud had imposed upon Tipú's credulity by leading him to believe that material assistance could be furnished from Mauritius, but they, naturally enough, concealed from their master the fact that he had been duped.

CHAPTER XII

Lord Mornington assumes the office of Governor-General—His Correspondence with Tipú

A new actor now appeared upon the scene. This was the justly-renowned Lord Mornington, who, with that keen instinct which is given to few, seized at a glance the real state of affairs, and by his judicious diplomacy and energetic action did more than any of his predecessors to place British power in India on a solid and sure foundation. He arrived at Madras just when Tipú's emissaries had come back from their fruitless expedition to Mauritius, and reached Calcutta in May, 1798. The next month he received intelligence of the Mysore embassy and Malartic's proclamation, and foreseeing that the aggressive tendency of the French Republic, then at war with all Europe, might impel it to send an army through Egypt to India, he adopted such precautionary measures as would prevent the native powers from coalescing with so formidable a rival. The first step in this direction was to negotiate with the Nizám for the dismissal of a French contingent amounting to

14,000 men, well-disciplined and ably commanded by the officers that had succeeded De Bussy in the Deccan. These troops were not only a defence against the Maráthás, but were hostile to the British, owing to the republican sympathies of their commander, M. Raymond, who carried on a secret correspondence with the Mysore sovereign. The Nizám distrusted both the English and Tipú. If he assented to the Governor-General's proposals and disbanded his French troops, he would lose the power of effectual resistance against the Maráthás, unless he leant on the support of the British Government, to whom he would in that case become subsidiary. If, on the other hand, he refused, and allied himself with Tipú, he would probably be overcome by the joint action of the two powers. On one side he regarded with apprehension the risk of disarming his French troops, and on the other the hostility of Tipú, with whom he had openly waged war, and whose advances towards a matrimonial alliance between the two sovereigns he had haughtily repelled. Swayed alternately by one or other of these considerations, it was long before the Nizám arrived at a decision. At last he consented to execute a treaty by which he agreed to disband his French troops, and to augment the English subsidiary force to six battalions and a due proportion of guns. The disarming was successfully effected, the Sepoys being taken into the English service, and the French officers sent, by way of England, to France.

With the Maráthás, Lord Mornington could not

hope for much success. While nominally participants in the treaty which Lord Cornwallis effected in 1790, the Maráthás had rendered little assistance in the first campaign. On the other hand, although Tipú had sent a special emissary to the Peshwá Bájí Ráo, adjuring him to get rid of Náná Farnavís, and urging an invasion of the Nizám's territory, he received in reply nothing but empty promises. Náná Farnavís though secretly hostile to the English, was too astute to relinquish his ascendancy over the Peshwá. He held aloof from any open recognition of either side, while Sindhia was averse from active military interference, striving only to prevent the Peshwá from giving full effect to the treaty of 1790. At the utmost, Lord Mornington could only expect, amidst these conflicting aims, that the Maráthás would observe a strict neutrality.

Fully aware of the danger which threatened the English from the ill-disguised hostility of Tipú, the Governor-General directed despatches to be sent early in June to the Madras Government, requesting them to consider the means of collecting a force should circumstances require it, and to state what number of men could be at once got together. The Madras Council vehemently remonstrated against any 'premature' attack upon the Mysore ruler, urging their disabled condition from the lack of supplies and draught-cattle, the low state of their finances, and previous failures. Even General Harris, the acting Governor, was to a great extent imbued with the same feeling. While expressing his readiness to carry out instructions, he deprecated hostilities which might end in discomfiture rather than in victory. Lord Mornington, however, was made of sterner metal. Knowing well how critical would be the state of affairs should a French expedition succeed in making its way from Egypt to India, he set aside these timorous objections, and insisted upon the Madras army being made ready for active operations, and put on a war-footing. On August 12, 1798, he recorded a minute in which, after adverting to Tipú's embassy to the Mauritius, and the clear proof of bad faith which it evinced, he remarked as follows :—

'Since the conclusion of the treaty of Seringapatam, the British Government in India have uniformly conducted themselves towards Tipú Sultán not only with the most exact attention to the principles of moderation, justice, and good faith, but have endeavoured by every practicable means to conciliate his confidence, and to mitigate his vindictive spirit. Some differences have occasionally arisen with respect to the boundaries of his territory bordering upon the confines of our possessions on the coast of Malabar, but the records of all the British Governments in India will show that they have always manifested the utmost anxiety to promote the amicable adjustment of every doubtful or disputed point, and that Tipú Sultán has received the most unequivocal proofs of the constant disposition of the Company to acknowledge and confirm all his just rights, and to remove every cause of jealousy, which might tend to interrupt the continuance of peace.'

Further on, in the same minute, after observing that

the Sultán's motive could only have been 'an ardent desire to expel the British nation from India,' he remarked:—

'If the conduct of Tipú Sultán had been of a nature which could be called ambiguous or suspicious; if he had merely increased his force beyond his ordinary establishment, or had stationed it in some position on our confines, or on those of our allies, which might justify jealousy or alarm; if he had renewed his secret intrigues at the courts of Haidarábád, Poona, and Cabul; or even if he had entered into any negotiation with France, of which the object was at all obscure; it might be our duty to resort in the first instance to his construction of proceedings which, being of a doubtful character, might admit of a satisfactory explanation. But where there is no doubt, there can be no matter for explanation. The act of Tipú's ambassadors, ratified by himself, and accompanied by the landing of a French force in his country, is a public, unqualified, and unambiguous declaration of war, aggravated by an avowal, that the object of the war is neither explanation, reparation, nor security, but the total destruction of the British Government in India.'

He concluded by saying:—

'This therefore is not merely the case of an injury to be repaired, but of the public safety to be secured against the present and future designs of an irreconcilable, desperate, and treacherous enemy. Against an enemy of this description no effectual security can be obtained, otherwise than by such a reduction of his power, as shall not only defeat his actual preparations, but establish a permanent restraint upon his future means of offence [1].'

[1] Fuller details of this statesmanlike minute, and of the motives

Lord Mornington, however, being averse from engaging unnecessarily in an expensive and uncertain campaign, had entered into a friendly correspondence with Tipú regarding certain claims preferred by that ruler to territory in Wainád (referred to in the first of the extracts above given), which, after due examination into the facts, he ordered to be surrendered to the Sultán. In writing to Tipú on November 8, 1798, Lord Mornington took the opportunity of referring, but in an amicable way, to Tipú's endeavour to bring about an alliance with the French, notwithstanding his repeated expressions of friendship for the English. He suggested that, in order to remove all causes of distrust, Major Doveton should be deputed to explain the Governor-General's views, and to establish cordial relations for the future. No answer was received to this proposal[1]. Lord Mornington then addressed to Tipú a second communication, pointing out the desirability of considering promptly the request made in his previous letter, and intimating that he was on the point of proceeding from Calcutta to Madras.

On November 20, 1798, before the first of these letters had reached him, Tipú wrote expressing his

which influenced the Governor-General's policy, will be found in Malleson's memoir of 'Wellesley.'

[1] The contemptuous way in which Tipú treated some of the Governor-General's letters, till compelled by circumstances to answer them, is a well-ascertained fact. The writer remembers seeing one of these communications, which had been preserved in the family of one of the Sultán's chief officers, and on which Tipú had endorsed 'jawáb na dárad,' i. e. 'no answer.'

astonishment that, in spite of his well-known friendship, the Governor-General meditated hostilities, adding that he discredited the report. On December 18 he wrote again, signifying his gratification at the defeat in Aboukir Bay of the French, whom he characterized as 'faithless, and the enemies of mankind.' But in regard to the proposed mission of Major Doveton, he evaded the suggestion, stating that existing treaties were sufficient. On January 9, 1799, Lord Mornington acknowledged the receipt of this communication, and recapitulated all the circumstances which had come to his notice regarding Tipú's open acts of hostility, again pressing for the reception of Major Doveton. A week afterwards Lord Mornington forwarded to Tipú a 'khat' from the Sublime Porte, in which Sultán Salím gave a full detail of the invasion of Egypt by the French, and stated that all true Musalmáns were bound to repel their aggressions. Tipú was specially requested to refrain from hostile proceedings against the English, or from lending a compliant ear to the French, and the Sublime Porte offered its good offices to adjust satisfactorily any cause of complaint. This important letter from the head of Islám was extremely disconcerting to the Mysore sovereign, who, on July 20, 1798, had addressed to the Executive Directory of the French Republic at Paris a despatch, soliciting an offensive and defensive alliance. Tipú sent as his ambassador Capitaine des Vaisseaux Dubuc, one of the two French officers who accompanied the small contingent forwarded from the

Isle of France to his assistance. On February 7, 1799, Monsieur Dubuc embarked at Tranquebar on his embassy. Yet Tipú, on the 16th of the same month, replied to the Sublime Porte in a grandiloquent despatch, full of professions of unbounded devotion for the head of his faith, winding up the strange epistle by saying:—

'As the French nation are estranged from, and are become the opponents of the Sublime Porte, they may be said to have rendered themselves the enemy of all the followers of the faith. All Musalmáns should renounce friendship with them.'

The above, however, was really only a pretended answer, intended to be forwarded through the Governor-General. In a separate communication, which Tipú forwarded by special means to Constantinople, he virulently attacked the English, as well as the French.

'All Hindustán,' he wrote, 'is overrun with Infidels and Polytheists, except the dominions of the Khudádád Sirkár (the God-given State), which, like the ark of Noah, are safe under the protection and bounteous aid of God.'

He proceeds to say that the English Governor-General (Lord Teignmouth) had caused Asaf-ud-dáulah, the Nawáb Vazír of Oudh, to be poisoned, had violated the chastity of his widow, and plundered his house of money and jewels to the amount of twenty crores of rupees. The wives and daughters of men of science and rank had been forcibly carried away by the English, and youthful descendants of the Prophet were compelled to eat the flesh of swine. He thus ended his tirade:—

> 'May the victorious banners of Islám ever prevail, and every trace of heresy and infidelity be swept away.'

No better proof could be adduced of the duplicity of the Sultán. To the Governor-General he wrote in a letter received on February 13:—

> 'As I am frequently going on sporting excursions, you had better send Major Doveton, regarding whom you have previously addressed me, slightly attended [1].'

[1] The actual Persian is 'jarídah rawánah báyad sákht,' which may mean slightly attended, or lightly equipped—at any rate implying that he attached no importance to the mission.

CHAPTER XIII

Lord Mornington declares War against Tipú—Final Siege of Seringapatam—The Sultán's Death

This insolent reply to Lord Mornington's overtures brought matters to a crisis. On February 22, 1799, the Governor-General issued a 'Declaration' on the part of the East India Company and their allies the Nizám and the Peshwá, in which he recounted the studious good faith of the British Government, and their anxiety to meet in every way the Sultán's reasonable demands, adducing as evidence of this the surrender of the territory claimed by him in Wainád—a concession which Tipú had himself admitted to be satisfactory. The document then goes on to relate the astonishment with which the allies discovered that, in spite of this evidence of their sincere adherence to the treaty of 1790, the Sultán had entered into negotiations with a hostile power for the purpose of commencing a war against the Company and the Allied Powers. It dwells upon the persistent delay on Tipú's part to receive an envoy to adjust existing grievances, and points out that this procrastination can only be attributed to his evident desire to protract the operations 'until some change of circumstance and of season shall revive his expectations of disturbing the tranquillity of India, by favouring the irruption of a French army.' The proclamation ends by saying that although the allies were resolved to ensure adequate protection against the danger which menaced them, they were still anxious to effect a friendly arrangement with the Sultán; and that General Harris, the Commander-in-Chief, had been empowered to receive any embassy which Tipú might despatch to headquarters to concert a treaty on such conditions as would lead to the establishment of a secure and permanent peace. A letter to like effect was on the same day transmitted to Tipú.

Although the Sultán's army was both smaller and inferior in discipline at this time, compared with what it was in 1792, it still amounted to about 33,000 infantry, 15,000 cavalry, and a strong body of artillery. The English army, which left Vellore on February 11 for the Mysore frontier, comprised 15,000 infantry, 2,600 cavalry, 600 European artillerymen, and 2,500 gun-lascars and pioneers, with 100 guns. To these must be added an efficient contingent from the Nizám, consisting of 6,500 of the subsidiary force, and 3,600 of the old French corps, with 6,000 horse, regular and irregular, bringing the total number of the united armies up to about 37,000 fighting men. Further, the army despatched from

Bombay under General Stuart amounted to 6,400 men, who, marching through the friendly country of Coorg, took up a position at the head of the Siddheshwar Pass, leading from that province into Mysore. On March 5, 1799, the Sultán, hearing of the approach of the Bombay force, suddenly made his appearance a few miles from Siddheshwar. Having drawn up his troops amounting to 12,000 men in three divisions, he marched under cover of the heavy jungle to attack the British advanced post of three battalions of Sepoys under the command of Lieutenant-Colonel Montresor. This brigade was completely surrounded, and would have been annihilated had it not been for the opportune arrival of General Stuart. The enemy then gave way and retreated, after losing many men, and one distinguished general, named Muhammad Razá, commonly called the Benki Nawáb or Fire-Nawáb[1]. General Stuart was accompanied on this occasion by Víraráj, the Wodiar of Coorg, who had rendered every assistance in his power to the British troops, and was present personally in the action.

Tipú now prepared to encounter the British army under General Harris, which had left Vellore, as mentioned, on February 11, and after reducing some

[1] The word 'Benki' in Kanarese literally means 'fire,' but signified in this case a man who carried fire and desolation into an enemy's country. It is stated of him that on one occasion he shut up certain rebellious Náirs, with their wives and children, in a house, and burned them alive. Muhammad Razá's descendants still reside in Mysore.

minor posts in the Báramahâls, had reached on March 9 Kellamangalam in Mysore. It was joined there by the Haidarábád contingent under Colonel Wellesley, and proceeded to an encampment near Bangalore. The progress made by it was very slow, owing to the multitude of camp-followers and cattle, which greatly impeded the march. Tipú had taken up a position near Maddúr, half-way between Bangalore and Seringapatam, but Lord Harris having determined to take the southerly route by Kánkánhalli, Tipú proceeded to encounter him near Malvalli, ten miles west of the Shimsha river. On March 27 the British army marched to this place and found the Mysore troops drawn up two miles from their intended encampment. Our advanced pickets were soon threatened by large bodies of cavalry, and when a corps was sent up to their support a general action ensued. Though Tipú's horse made a gallant attack, and his finest infantry advanced firmly against the 33rd regiment, they were charged with the bayonet and driven back in confusion. The English cavalry completed their rout, and destroyed nearly all of them. Tipú then withdrew his guns and troops, having lost 1,000 men killed and wounded in the engagement, while the British loss was trifling.

The mistake of Tipú in supposing that the British army would take the direct road from Bangalore to Seringapatam, and attack that place from the north, as Lord Cornwallis had done in 1792, was of immense service to Lord Harris. Under this anticipation,

Tipú had ordered the destruction of all forage on the more direct route, which he held in force. But the English general, by marching to the south and crossing the Káveri at Sosilé, not only found ample fodder, but effected the passage of the ford without opposition. He was now within fifteen miles of Seringapatam, and Tipú found out that all his efforts to prevent the enemy from reaching within striking distance of his capital had been completely frustrated. He then consulted his leading officers as to the best course to pursue, and, according to their advice, resolved to give battle near the Chendgal ford, by which they calculated that the British force would cross over to the island of Seringapatam. All his Sardárs vowed to sacrifice their lives if necessary in the expected combat, and Tipú sending his two eldest sons into the fort to defend it to the last, crossed the river with his army to take up a position at Chendgal to meet the expected foe. To his dismay, however, he found that the British commander, instead of proceeding to the right as he had anticipated, deviated to the left, in order to avoid some intervening low ground. On April 3 our force reached the position in which General Abercromby had encamped in 1792, on the south-west side of the island.

During the time which had intervened since Lord Cornwallis' siege of Seringapatam, the Sultán had given great attention to strengthening the fortifications. But, excepting a battery which he had erected on the north-west angle of the fort, his improvements had been mainly directed to the south and east sides. The works on the west side where the wall overlooks the Káveri were not so strong, although even here they were protected by a double wall and a ditch. In front of the British army was broken rising ground, with some deserted villages, and several topes or groves of areca-nut palms and cocoa trees, which afforded a safe cover to Tipú's skirmishers and rocket-men, and enabled them to harass the English pickets. One of these groves, called the Sultánpet Tope, was intersected by deep ditches, watered from a channel running in an easterly direction about a mile from the fort. General Baird was directed to scour this grove and dislodge the enemy, but on his advancing with this object on the night of the 5th, he found the tope unoccupied. The next day, however, the Mysore troops again took possession of the ground, and as it was absolutely necessary to expel them, two columns were detached at sunset for the purpose. The first of these, under Colonel Shawe, got possession of a ruined village, which it successfully held. The second column, under Colonel Wellesley, on advancing into the tope, was at once attacked in the darkness of night by a tremendous fire of musketry and rockets. The men, floundering about amidst the trees and the water-courses, at last broke, and fell back in disorder, some being killed and a few taken prisoners. In the confusion Colonel Wellesley was himself struck on the knee by a spent ball, and narrowly escaped falling into the hands of the enemy[1]. The next day, however, a detachment under his command succeeded in taking possession of the grove, and General Harris was enabled to proceed with his siege-operations, the army taking up its final position on April 7, 1799.

On the 9th, the Sultán, alarmed at the state of affairs, sent an agent to the English general's camp with a letter, inquiring the meaning of the hostile proceedings against him, and asserting his own adherence to existing treaties. General Harris in his reply contented himself with referring Tipú to Lord Mornington's letter of February 22, and continued to prosecute the siege. On April 14, the Bombay army joined the headquarters with abundant supplies, and two days afterwards took up a strong position on the northern bank of the Káveri. During the ensuing week, numerous batteries were erected, several important outposts were seized, and a determined attack by a strong body of infantry, led by French officers[2], against the advanced posts of the Bombay army, was repulsed with great loss.

On the 20th, Tipú again expressed a wish for a conference to adjust the terms of a peace. General Harris, acting on the plenary powers with which he

[1] This grove, which has an historical interest, as being one of the very few places where the famous Duke met with a repulse, may still be seen in the vicinity of Seringapatam. A more detailed account of the disaster will be found in *The Life of Sir David Baird*. For accurate details of the siege itself, the reader is referred to Colonel A. Beatson's work, published in 1800.

[2] The whole number of French at this time in the Sultán's service was only 120, including 20 officers.

had been entrusted, forwarded the draft of a preliminary treaty for his acceptance. This document stipulated that the Sultán should at once dismiss all Frenchmen in his service; that he should cede half his territory to the allies; pay two millions sterling, half immediately, and the remainder in six months; release all his prisoners; and finally make over as hostages two of his eldest sons [1], besides four of his chief officers, whose names were given. A term of twenty-four hours only was allowed for the Sultán's assent to these conditions. No answer was received to these demands, and the siege being uninterruptedly proceeded with, all the guns on the west face of the fort were silenced by the 24th. The west cavalier and north-west bastion were dismantled, and the fire of the enemy was reduced to a few guns on the south face, and some distant cavaliers. On the 26th and 27th hard fighting took place, in order to dislodge the Mysore troops from an exterior entrenchment still held by them, which impeded the erection of breaching batteries, and was protected on one side by a redoubt, and on the other by a circular work that afforded a flanking defence. After an obstinate contest, in which the enemy behaved with great bravery, all these obstacles were carried, and the Mysore troops were forced to retreat beyond the river.

[1] In the letter to Tipú of April 22, four sons are mentioned, namely, Sultán Pádsháh, Fatah Haidar, Moíz-ud-dín, and Abd-ul-Khálik.

The Sultán, now in despair, again attempted to open negotiations, and on the 28th wrote intimating his wish to send ambassadors to confer with the English general. He was told in reply that the allies would only treat on the basis of the conditions already forwarded to him, and that no envoys would be received unless accompanied by the hostages and specie required. This was the end of Tipú's abortive attempts to avert the ruin which was about to befall him [1].

On May 2, all the batteries having been completed were unmasked. They opened a heavy fire on the western curtain of the fort, about sixty yards south-east of the bastion on the western angle, and a practicable breach having been effected on the evening of the next day, orders were issued for an assault at 1 p.m. on the 4th. Tipú, a prey to despair in the imminent peril which threatened him, condescended, in spite of his orthodox Islámism, to have recourse to the prayers and incantations of the Bráhmans whom he had hitherto invariably despised and ill-treated. But although he heaped rich gifts upon them, they were either too honest or too wise to predict a successful escape from the fate which was following him. Dressed in a light-coloured jacket, with trousers of fine chintz, a red silk sash, a rich turban, and an

[1] It was about this time that thirteen English soldiers, who had been taken prisoners, were killed by the Sultán's orders, their necks being twisted by the professional executioners called Jettis, the native gladiators of the south of India.

embroidered belt, with a talisman on his right arm, he proceeded early on the 4th to his headquarters in a gateway on the northern face, called the Kaḷḷa Diḍḍi, or private sally-port. Shortly after his arrival at this post, he was informed of the death from a cannon-shot of Sayyad Ghafúr, one of his most trusty officers, who was struck down while gallantly heading the troops in the breach. Soon afterwards a report was brought to him of the actual assault.

The command of the storming party had been entrusted to General Baird, the same officer who had languished for more than three years in the dungeons of Seringapatam, having been taken prisoner after Baillie's defeat at Perambákam in 1780. This gallant soldier, full of energy and animated by the recollection of the ill-usage to which he and his companions in arms had been ruthlessly subjected, stepped out of the trenches, and drawing his sword, called out to his men: 'Now, my brave fellows, follow me, and prove yourselves worthy of the name of British soldiers.' In an instant, his troops rushed forward, and crossed the river in six minutes, under a tremendous fire of musketry and rockets from the enemy. The forlorn hope was confronted on the slope of the breach by a small body of the Mysore troops who offered a determined opposition, but they were soon struck down, and in a few minutes the British flag was hoisted on the ramparts. The Sultán hastened towards the breach, and endeavoured to rally his soldiers, encouraging them to make a stand.

He repeatedly fired on the assailants, but the rapid approach of the English column, and the desertion of his followers, compelled him to retreat. The greater part of the English troops had proceeded along the ramparts, filing off to the right and left, in obedience to orders, but a portion of the 12th regiment pressed forward into the town, and, keeping along the inside of the rampart, found themselves opposite the sally-port, through which the Sultán proposed returning. On his arriving at a bridge leading to the inner fort, he mounted his horse, and endeavoured to enter the town, but on reaching the gate the passage was so crowded by fugitives that he was unable to pass.

While his progress was thus hampered, his pursuers fired into the gateway, and wounded him in the breast. He pushed on, however, but was stopped by the fire of the soldiers of the 12th regiment from inside the gate, receiving a second wound in the right side, while his horse fell under him. He was immediately raised by some of his faithful attendants, and placed in his palankeen under an arch in the gateway. He was implored to make himself known to the English troops, from whose commanders he would no doubt have received the attention due to his rank, but he absolutely refused to comply with the suggestion. Soon afterwards some European soldiers entered the gateway, one of whom attempted to take off his richly-jewelled sword-belt, when Tipú, sorely wounded as he was, made a cut at the man, and wounded him in the knee. The enraged soldier levelled his musket and shot him in the head, causing instantaneous death. A considerable time elapsed before any authentic intelligence of the Sultán's fate was obtained; but the British troops being now in possession of every part of the ramparts, and opposition having ceased, General Baird proceeded to make inquiries as to what had become of him.

Major Allan, Deputy Quartermaster-General, was accordingly sent to the palace with a flag of truce to demand the surrender of Tipú, and after some delay ascertained that a report had been received there that he had been wounded at the gate above-mentioned. On repairing thither at dusk, the body of the Sultán was, after much labour, discovered in a heap of slain, and clearly identified. It was still warm, and the eyes were open, the countenance being in no way distorted, although there were three wounds in the body and one in the temple. His turban, jacket, and sword-belt had disappeared, but the talisman on his right arm, containing an amulet with Arabic characters on the manuscript inside, was at once recognized. The body was placed in his palankeen, and, by General Baird's orders, conveyed to the palace for the night.

The next day the funeral cortége, escorted by four companies of Europeans, proceeded from the fortress to the Lál Bágh, where the remains of the ambitious and unfortunate sovereign were interred by the side of his father, Haidar Alí. The bier was borne by his personal attendants, and followed by Prince Abd-ul-

Khálik and the principal officers of the court, the streets through which the procession passed being crowded by Musalmáns, who prostrated themselves, and evinced every sign of grief. On reaching the gate of the mausoleum the troops presented arms, the Kázi read the funeral service, and when the body had been deposited in the tomb, a donation of 12,000 rupees was made to the religious men and poor people who attended the obsequies. It is related that the solemnity of the ceremony was enhanced by terrific claps of thunder which burst over the island immediately afterwards.

The sons of the late Sultán were made prisoners, and such of them as had arrived at maturity were sent with their families to Vellore, whence some years afterwards, owing to their having been accused of instigating the troops to mutiny in 1806, they were transported to Calcutta. Many persons still remember the venerable Prince Ghulám Muhammad, one of the younger sons, who died a few years ago. He was greatly respected as a Justice of Peace, and for his hospitality and charity. One of his last acts was to establish a fund for poor and deserving persons in Mysore.

To the honour of General Baird it must be mentioned that, mainly owing to his humane efforts, there was little effusion of blood after Seringapatam was taken, notwithstanding the prolonged resistance and his remembrance of his own sufferings. Safeguards were sent to the houses of all the principal chiefs, who, finding that their property and the honour of their families were respected, readily submitted to the conquerors. Steps were also taken to secure the property in the palace, but the discovery of a private entrance into the treasury enabled marauders to carry off a vast amount of coin and jewellery before they could be stopped. Nevertheless, what remained was of priceless value. A magnificent throne, a superb howdah, curious and richly-jewelled matchlocks and swords, solid gold and silver plate, costly carpets and china ware, a profusion of fine gems, and a valuable library, were among the treasures found in the palace[1].

In this memorable siege no fewer than 8,000 of the Mysore troops are said to have perished. On the British side, 892 Europeans were killed or wounded, of whom 65 were officers, and of the native troops

[1] The specie alone amounted to sixteen lacs of pagodas, or £480,000, while the jewels were valued at nine lacs. The total number of ordnance captured was 929, including guns, mortars, and howitzers, 176 of which were twelve-pounders and over. The library contained many curious and interesting manuscripts, of which the following is a summary:—Korán, 44 vols.; Commentaries on Korán, 41; Prayers, 35; Traditions, 46; Theology, 46; Súfyism (mystic writings), 115; Ethics, 24; Jurisprudence, 95; Arts and Sciences, 19; Philosophy, 54; Astronomy, 20; Mathematics, 7; Physic, 62; Philology, 45; Lexicography, 29; History, 118; Letters, 53; Poetry, 190; Hindí and Deccani Poetry, 23; Hindí and Deccani Prose, 4; Turkish Prose, 2; Fables, 18. Some of these books belonged to the Kings of Bíjápur and Golconda, but the majority were plundered at Chittúr, Sávanúr, and Kadapa. With the exception of one precious Korán, which was forwarded to Windsor Castle, the greater part of this library was transferred to the newly-founded College at Fort William, Calcutta.

639. Estimating the total number of Europeans engaged (including two regiments with the Bombay army) at about 7,000, and the native troops (exclusive of the Nizám's contingent) at 20,000, this would show that the proportionate loss in the ranks of the former was about four times that in the native troops. The fact may be attributed in great measure to the heavy loss among the Europeans in the actual assault.

It is not within the scope of this narrative to detail the steps taken by Lord Mornington after the fall of Seringapatam. It may perhaps suffice to say that they evinced in an uncommon degree political sagacity, sound judgment, and generosity. The claims of our allies, the Nizám and the Maráthás, were duly considered. To revive a hostile power in the person of one of Tipú's sons was clearly inadvisable, and the question therefore arose as to how to dispose of the conquered territory. The solution which the Governor-General arrived at was to divide part of the Sultán's dominions between the allies. The British Government received a territory yielding 537,000 Kánthirái pagodas[1], and including all the western coast, while to the Nizám were allotted

[1] These pagodas were originally struck by Rájá Kánthirái (1638–58), six of them equalling five star pagodas. The native name for this coin is 'varáha,' or 'boar,' one of the incarnations of Vishnu, which was the crest of some of the older Mysore dynasties. The word pagoda is a Portuguese name for the coin, and a supposed corruption of the Persian 'but-kadah,' an idol temple, many of the pagodas showing a temple on the obverse face. [But see Jule's *Glossary* for a discussion of its possible derivations.] The intrinsic value is about three rupees.

districts producing a like amount, and to the Peshwá districts yielding 264,000 pagodas. The remainder of the late ruler's possessions, with a revenue estimated at 1,374,100 pagodas, and exceeding in area the whole Mysore kingdom when Haidar Alí usurped the rule in 1761, was bestowed as a free gift on the infant son of the last Mysore Rájá, Chámráj, who died in 1796, on condition that an annual subsidy of seven lacs of star pagodas should be paid to the British Government, that a general control over the affairs of Mysore should be exercised by a Resident at his court, and that the island of Seringapatam should be ceded to the British Government in perpetuity. These liberal conditions were gratefully acknowledged by the widow of Chikka Krishnaráj and the widow of Chámráj in the following letter, dated June 24, 1799:—

'Your having conferred on our child the government of Mysore, Nagar, and their dependencies, and appointed Púrnaiya to be the Diwán, has afforded us the greatest happiness. Forty years have elapsed since our government ceased. Now you have favoured our boy with the government of this country, and nominated Púrnaiya to be his Diwán. We shall, while the sun and moon continue, commit no offence against your government. We shall at all times consider ourselves as under your protection and orders. Your having established us must for ever be fresh in the memory of our posterity, from one generation to another. Our offspring can never forget an attachment to your government, on whose support we shall depend.

Signed, LACHHMI AMMANI.
DÉWAJÍ AMMANI.'

The youthful Rájá was accordingly duly installed, and after a long reign, the latter part of which was embittered by the consciousness of sovereign duties but ill performed, died in 1868, deeply regretted by all who knew his kindly but somewhat facile character. The Commissioners appointed to carry out the Governor-General's instructions allotted handsome pensions to the Sultán's principal officers, who testified in lively terms their appreciation of this wholly unexpected generosity.

To an Englishman few places in India are more replete with interesting historical associations than Seringapatam. At the extreme eastern end of the island is the famous mausoleum of Haidar Alí, where also repose the remains of his ill-starred son. The tomb stands on a raised terrace at the end of an avenue of cypress trees, with an arcade all round it, and a mosque on the right-hand side. It is a square building, surmounted by a dome, and supported by polished black marble columns, which are very handsome, all the rest being pure white, and adorned with fine carvings. The doors are of ebony, inlaid with ivory (the gift of Lord Dalhousie), and at the principal entrance hangs a scarlet curtain embroidered with gold. Inside are the two tombs of Haidar and Tipú, each of them covered by a splendid Kashmír shawl, worked in rich patterns. Peacocks' feathers and other insignia of royalty lie about on the floor, while incense is burnt in a niche. The building is maintained at the Government expense.

Although not so striking as the famous mausoleums to be seen in Upper India and at Ahmadábád and elsewhere, it is a fine monument. It presents a sad contrast to the graves of the English officers and men who fell at Seringapatam, and who are laid in an adjacent cemetery, the ground overgrown by weeds, and the names on the ugly flat stones barely distinguishable [1].

On the southern side of the left branch of the Káveri, and midway between the Lál Bágh and the fort, is the picturesque Daryá Dáulat Bágh, or 'garden of the wealth of the sea,' for many months the residence of England's greatest soldier (the Duke of Wellington). It was a favourite resort of Tipú, being near the fortress, and is of elegant design. The walls inside are covered with richly-painted arabesques, while outside are a series of frescos representing the triumphs of Tipú over the English. The most remarkable of these designs is intended to delineate the defeat of Baillie at Perambákam, and is a most amusing caricature, that General being shown reclining helplessly in a palankeen, while Tipú on horseback is calmly smelling a rose and giving orders to his troops. The perspective is ludicrous—legs, arms, and heads flying off in all

[1] The writer made an attempt to remedy the neglect to which these memorials had been exposed. But the lapse of time and the effects of an Indian climate, added to the rough character of the tombstones and the difficulty of identifying the names on them, rendered any real restoration well-nigh impossible.

directions, and considerable research is needed to find the corresponding bodies. These frescos were effaced by Tipú before the siege, but restored by Colonel Wellesley when he inhabited the building. In course of time they again became hardly recognizable, when Lord Dalhousie, on his visit to Mysore in 1854, ordered them to be repainted by a native artist.

The old fortress of Seringapatam remains in much the same state as it was left in after the siege nearly a hundred years ago. The formidable fortifications have stoutly withstood the ravages of time, while the breach made in the curtain is still visible from the opposite bank of the river, where two cannons fixed in the ground denote the spot on which the English batteries were erected. Inside is shown the gateway on the northern face where Tipú fell in his death-struggle. The whole island is now insalubrious. A few wretched houses only remain where once was a great capital, and the ancient temple of Vishnu looks down, as if in mockery, on the ruins of the palace of the Muhammadan usurper[1].

[1] Part of the building has been demolished, and the rest turned into a sandal-wood store.

CHAPTER XIV

TIPÚ'S CHARACTER AND ADMINISTRATION—HIS FANATICISM AND CRUELTY

THE character of Tipú stands out in marked contrast to that of his more celebrated father. Personal courage he certainly possessed, and he is said to have been a good rider and a skilful marksman. Although deficient in the capacity for war which eminently distinguished Haidar, he on several occasions showed considerable skill in strategy: for example, in his success over Colonel Braithwaite, his campaign against the Maráthás in 1786, his many encounters with General Medows, and his rapid movements in South Arcot. Had he trusted more to his cavalry as his most efficient mode of attack, he might have obtained greater successes in the field than he actually secured, but his overweening confidence in his own generalship and knowledge of tactics was often the cause of disaster and defeat to his armies.

It has already been mentioned that in 1786 Tipú assumed the title of Pádsháh or King, and in referring to his own person began to call himself 'the resplendent presence,' and 'our prosperous person,' while his army was denoted as 'the holy camp.' The same inflated ideas of his royal dignity appear in the titles which he gave to his government, such as 'the God-given state,' 'the Lion of God government,' 'the Haidarí rule,' &c. But he was very chary of bestowing titular honours on his own chief officials, whose respectful salutations he never deigned to acknowledge. In addressing even great foreign potentates, such as the King of France, he used expressions only suitable when writing to an inferior. The climax of his arrogance was reached when he ordered the 'Khutbah,' or daily prayer in the mosques, to be read in his own name, instead of that of the Mughal Emperor.

He had a rage for innovations, and was constantly changing the names of places, and altering well-established customs. To natives of India who, like most Orientals, delight to 'stand in the old paths,' many of the changes introduced by the English, though in themselves generally beneficial and often laudable, are distasteful in the extreme. The fanciful innovations of Tipú were the effect of mere caprice. He must needs alter the territorial divisions of his dominions, calling the coast districts the 'Yam Súba,' the ancient Malnád the 'Taran Súba,' and the plain country the 'Ghabra Súba.'

In like manner innumerable changes were made in the names of places, the town of Devanhalli, where he was born, being called Yusafábád, the abode of

Joseph, the fairest of men. Chitaldrúg was changed to Farukh-yáb Hisár, or the 'propitiously-acquired castle;' Gútti to Fáiz Hisár, or the 'citadel of grace,' and so forth; but, as may be supposed, all these places have relapsed into their old names. Measures of distance too were amended, the *kos* or Indian two-miles being now defined as consisting of so many yards of twice twenty-four thumb-breadths, because the creed (Kalmah) contains twenty-four letters. The *kos* thus fixed was $2\frac{3}{4}$ miles, and if the letter-carriers did not travel this distance in $33\frac{3}{4}$ minutes they were to be flogged. All the names of weights and measures were altered. But the most wonderful of his improvements was his new method of calculating time. As is well known, the Hindus counted time in cycles of 60 years, each year having a separate name, a system which makes their chronology somewhat difficult to unravel. Tipú founded a new calendar on this basis, giving however fantastic names to the years, and equally strange ones to the lunar months. The year, according to his arrangement, only contained 354 days, and each month was called by some name in alphabetical order. From the year 1784, all his letters were dated according to the day of one or other of the months in this new nomenclature.

It may be remarked that his pen was most prolific, and that he condescended to write to his officials, both civil and military, detailed instructions on every conceivable matter, whether the question before him related to military operations, general regulations, or even petty trading. He pronounced decided opinions on science, medicine, commerce, religious observances, engineering, military establishments, and a host of abstruse matters with equal facility, but with little real knowledge[1]. He seems to have written Persian with tolerable readiness, signing his name generally in a device or cryptogram, meaning 'Nabbi Málik,' or 'the Prophet is Master[2].' He was assiduous in his correspondence, and had little leisure for pastimes. He wrote to a certain Tarbíyat Alí Khán, 'That great person' (used here contemptuously for the correspondent addressed) 'eats two or three times a day, sits at his ease, and amuses himself with talk, whereas we are occupied from morning to night with business.' There can be no doubt about his business habits, and his

[1] Tipú laid claim to universal knowledge, but was certainly eclipsed by the famous Dane, Archbishop Absalon, who died in 1202. This really accomplished man was Prime Minister, Commander-in-Chief, Lord High Admiral, and was versed in all kinds of learning. He was an excellent adviser to his King, and employed his spare moments in chopping billets of wood. Cf. Holberg's *Dannemark's Historie*, vol. i. p. 186.

[2] The writer possesses an order of his dated 2d Bahári of the year Shádáb, 1226, Máulúd, that is, the birth of Muhammad (not the era of the Flight or Hijri), but it is probable that this newly-formed era really had reference to the period when the Prophet first announced himself as the messenger of God. The order in question bears the signature, 'Nabbi Málik.' Another order with the same signature has also on it a square seal with the impression 'Tipú Sultán.' It has been said that the title of Fatah Alí Khán was bestowed upon him by the Emperor Sháh Álam, but the writer is not aware whether he made use of this in his official correspondence.

correspondence was registered with great regularity and precision, judging from the records found at Seringapatam.

One of Tipú's flights of fancy was the issue of a new coinage bearing on the obverse 'the faith of Ahmad (Muhammad) is proclaimed to the world by the victories of Haidar—struck in Patan (Seringapatam) in the year Jalú or 1199 Hijri:' and on the reverse 'He (either God or Tipú?) is the only Sultán, the just one—the third of Bahári in the year Jalú, and third of the reign.' He had the audacity to send an offering of these coins, in which, contrary to received usage, the name of the Emperor was studiously omitted, to Sháh Álam. When he found that the Great Mughal took offence at the inscription, he pretended that he had merely sent the coins in order to ascertain His Majesty's pleasure about them, and offered an apology for the affront.

As he claimed an intimate acquaintance with all military matters, he compiled a code called 'The Triumphs of Holy Warriors,' a work in eighteen chapters. Minute instructions are given in it for guidance regarding manual exercises, the duties of all grades of officers, night attacks, fighting in a wooded country or on plains, salutes on special occasions, military guards, furlough, desertions, and so forth. According to an ordinance (Hukmnámah) issued by the Sultán in 1793, the 'Piádah Askar,' or regular infantry, then comprised five Kachahris or divisions, and twenty-seven Kashúns[1] or regiments, each Kashún containing 1,392 men (of whom 1,056 carried muskets) with a suitable staff, combatant and non-combatant. A Jáuk, or company of rocket-men, was attached to each Kashún, and also two guns. The cavalry force was divided into three establishments—(1) Regular Cavalry, (2) Silahdárs, who provided their own horses, and (3) Kazzáks, or Predatory Cavalry. Of these the first, called 'Sawár Askar,' comprised three Kachahris or divisions, consisting each of six Mokabs or regiments of 376 troopers. The Silahdárs mustered 6,000 horse, and the Kazzáks 8,000.

Nor did the necessity for maintaining a fleet escape the vigilant eye of Tipú Sultán. His ordinance on the subject, although merely a paper edict which was never carried into effect, is not a little curious. In 1796 a Board of Admiralty, consisting of eleven persons, was nominated under the appellation of Mír Yam, or sea-lords, under whom were to be thirty Mír Bahar or commanders of the fleet. The navy was to consist of twenty line-of-battle ships, and twenty large frigates, of which six of each class were to be stationed at Jamálábád or Mangalore, seven of each at Wájidábád near the Mirján creek,

[1] The word Kashún or Kshún, though adopted into the Persian language, is apparently derived from the Sanskrit 'Aksháuhini,' but had formerly a much more extended signification. The 'Kshúns' mentioned in the Mahábhárata, each comprised 2,730 elephants, 2,730 chariots, 7,290 horsemen, and 12,150 foot.

and seven at Májídábád or Sadáshivgarh. The line-of-battle ships were divided into first and second class. The former were to mount seventy-two guns, the latter sixty-two of three different classes of calibre, while the frigates were to carry forty-six guns. The Sultán kindly sent a model to the Admiralty Board for their guidance in building the ships, ordering them to have copper bottoms, and prescribing where the timber for them was to be cut. Minute details were furnished as to the complement of the ships, and the pay of all grades. It was amusingly ordered that twenty of the Mír Bahar, or those highest in rank, were to receive a horse allowance, and that when the Mír Yam visited the fleet, they should get a specially good dinner, with fruit, at the expense of the Government. This grand scheme for creating a navy came to nothing. Before the ships could be built the Sultán's rule was extinguished.

Tipú showed his orthodoxy as a good Musalmán in strictly prohibiting the sale of intoxicating drinks. Although his method of proceeding was somewhat arbitrary, and he cared little about 'local option,' it must be admitted that in this department he showed himself a sensible reformer. He did indeed permit M. Lally to open one shop in his camp for the vending of spirituous liquors, but he firmly restricted the use of it to the French soldiers in his service. In writing to the local official at Bangalore in 1787, Tipú directed him to take written engagements from both the vendors and distillers of intoxicating drinks to give up their profession and take to some other occupation. Similar orders were issued throughout his territory.

In 1786 he issued a remarkable proclamation, calling upon all true believers to 'extract the cotton of negligence from the ears of their understanding,' and, quitting the territories of apostates[1] and unbelievers, to take refuge in his dominions, where, by the Divine blessing, they would be better provided for than before, and their lives, honour, and property remain under the protection of God. He was resolved that the worthless and stiff-necked infidels, who had turned aside their heads from obedience to the true faith, and openly raised the standard of unbelief, should be chastised by the hands of the faithful, and made either to acknowledge the true religion or to pay tribute. As, owing to the imbecility of the princes of Hind, that insolent race (presumably the English) had conceived the futile opinion that true believers had become weak, mean, and contemptible, and had overrun and laid waste the territories of Musalmáns, extending the hand of violence and injustice on the property and honour of the faithful, he had resolved to prosecute a holy war against them. This virulent tirade, although its dissemina-

[1] He professed to regard the Nizám as an apostate, because he had at various times sided with the English and the Maráthás, and did not hesitate to apply abusive epithets to him, such as 'barber' and 'son of a worthless mother.'

tion was at first confined to his own dominions, was afterwards transmitted by his orders to various places in the Nizám's territory, with the object of inducing all true believers to join his standard, and to aid him in exterminating the English from India. In writing to the Mughal Emperor in the previous year he said:—

'This steadfast believer, with a view to the support of the firm religion of Muhammad, undertook the chastisement of the Nazarene tribe, who, unable to maintain the war I waged against them, solicited peace in the most abject manner. With the divine aid and blessing of God, it is now again my steady determination to set about the total extirpation and destruction of the enemies of the faith.'

He apparently took little heed about disguising his real sentiments, although at the same time carrying on a professedly amicable correspondence with the English Government. But of his habitual duplicity there are ample proofs. For example, when his troops were besieging the fort of Nargúnd, previously mentioned, he instructed his commander Búrhán-ud-dín to temporize, and employ every means, 'fair or foul,' to induce the besieged to surrender the place.

Allusion has been made in a previous chapter to the wholesale deportation of the unfortunate people of Coorg. The Sultán in his memoirs gives the following account of his proceedings at Zafírábád, as he chose to call Merkára, the capital:—

'It is the custom with you for the eldest of five brothers to marry, and for the wife of such brother to be common to all five: hence there cannot be the slightest doubt of your all being bastards. This is about the seventh time that you have acted treacherously towards the Government, and plundered our armies. I have now vowed to the true God that if you ever again conduct yourselves traitorously or wickedly, I will not revile or molest a single individual among you, but making Ahmadis (Musalmáns) of the whole of you, transplant you all from this country to some other; by which means, from being illegitimate, your progeny or descendants may become legitimate, and the epithet of "sons of sinful mothers" may no longer belong to your tribe.'

This expression of his ideas was not dictated by any tender feeling for women in general. A letter to Búrhán-ud-dín in 1786, in which he directs Búrhán to cross the Tungábhadra from Anavatti, runs thus: 'You must leave the women and other rubbish, together with the superfluous baggage of your army, behind.' In fact, the Sultán, though he left a dozen sons behind him, does not appear to have been, like his father, very susceptible to the charms of the fair sex. He deemed women of little account, with the sole exception of his mother whose influence over him was great.

There is little to say about Tipú's revenue administration, which, owing to his frequent wars and his absence from his capital, naturally fell into the hands of his subordinates. Although the old system of collecting the Government dues which was in force in the time of the Hindu Rájás was still preserved, the want of proper supervision led to numerous exactions and consequent discontent, of which he remained in ignorance. Of regular judicial procedure there was little or no trace. Every amildár, or district officer, acted much as he pleased: to complain against oppression was dangerous. In one department, however, the Sultán took a special interest, owing to the deep distrust which he entertained even against his principal officials, whose families were compelled to reside permanently at the capital. In order to ascertain what went on in their households, the police were directed 'to place spies in the fort, in the town of Ganjám adjoining it, in the bazárs, and over the doors of the great Mírs, so as to gain intelligence of every person who went to another's house and of what was said, thereby acquiring an accurate knowledge of the true state of things, to be reported daily to the Presence.' It was at the same time forbidden that any one should go to the house of another to converse [1].

Of Tipú's ferocious character there are unfortunately abundant proofs, some of which may be mentioned in addition to what has already been said on this subject. As they are taken from his own correspondence there can be no doubt as to their authenticity. In one letter, written during the progress of the siege of Nargúnd, he says:—

'In the event of your being obliged to assault the place,

[1] Latterly, the Sultán appears to have neglected the duties of his State, and to have allowed the control of affairs to remain in the hands of worthless inferiors, while he passed his time in prayer, reading the Korán, and counting the beads of his Tasbíh or rosary.

every living creature in it, whether man or woman, old or young, child, dog, cat, or anything else, must be put to the sword, with the single exception of Kála Pandit (the commandant)—what more?'

In another, addressed to an officer in Coorg, he remarks:—

'You are to make a general attack on the Coorgs, and, having put to the sword or made prisoners the whole of them, both the *slain* and the prisoners, with the women and children, are to be made Musalmáns [1].'

Again, alluding to a rising at Súpa in Kánara, he writes to Badr-uz-zamán Khán:—

'Ten years ago, from ten to fifteen thousand men were hung upon the trees of that district; since which time the aforesaid trees have been waiting for more men. You must therefore hang upon trees all such of the inhabitants of that district as have taken a lead in these rebellious proceedings.'

In another letter, despatched to Arshad Bég Khán at Calicut respecting certain highway robbers, he says:—

'Such of the authors of this rebellion and flagrant conduct as have been already killed, are killed. But why should the remainder of them, on being made prisoners, be put to death? Their proper punishment is this: Let the dogs, both black and white, be regularly despatched to Seringapatam [2].'

Again he writes regarding some of the Nizám's

[1] In the original Persian, 'Kasáníkih kushtah shudand wa kasáníkih asír shuwand, máh zan wa bachah, hamahhárá musalmán namáyand.'

[2] This is significant of what imprisonment at Seringapatam foreshadowed. The word 'white' is supposed to apply to the Christian portion of these people.

cavalry, of whom six had been taken prisoners at Kadapa:—

'Let the prisoners be strangled, and the horses, after being valued, be taken into Government service.'

But enough has been said to show the character of a ruler, who urged on by religious bigotry, innate cruelty, and despotism, thought little of sacrificing thousands of lives to his ardent zeal and revengeful feelings. These darker shades in his disposition are not relieved by any evidence of princely generosity, such as Haidar Alí occasionally showed. Tipú would grumble at the expense of clothing his troops, or even at the number of wax-candles needed for ship-stores. He once rebuked an officer who complained of being supplied with old and black rice, by telling him not to engage in improper altercation.

Whatever indignation may be excited by the Sultán's vindictive character, it is enhanced by the miserable state of the prisoners who fell into his hands. Haidar indeed put his captives in irons, fed them sparingly, and treated them badly, but he rarely took their lives deliberately. Tipú, on the other hand, had no compunction in cutting their throats, or strangling and poisoning them; while, as has been stated, numbers of them were sent to die of malaria and starvation on the fatal mountain of Kabáldrúg. The English prisoners were specially selected as victims of his vengeance, not omitting officers of rank such as General Matthews; while, in direct contravention of the treaty made at Mangalore in 1784, he did not scruple to retain in captivity considerable numbers of Europeans. Many of these, particularly young and good-looking boys, were forcibly circumcised, married haphazard to girls who had been captured in the Coromandel districts, and drafted into the ranks of the army, or compelled to sing and dance for the amusement of the sovereign.

It must be admitted that the times were barbarous, and that the most atrocious punishments were frequently inflicted on malefactors. Even impaling was occasionally resorted to[1], and it would be unjust to attribute to Tipú alone the commission of crimes which were characteristic of the period. It has been mentioned that those who conspired against him were put in a cage. This was an imitation of Haidar's treatment of Khande Ráo. The unhappy victims were allowed half a pound of rice a day, with salt, but no water, so they soon expired under this frightful ordeal. There were other punishments nearly equally dreadful, such as making men bestride a wooden horse on a saddle studded with sharp spikes. On a spring being touched the horse of torture reared, and the spikes penetrated the unfortunate wretches. A more common mode of punishment was to bind tightly the hands

[1] The writer was shown at Bednúr the Shúla Battery Hill, where one can still see the hole in the ground in which was inserted the stake (shúla) for impaling victims, who were then hoisted and held up *in terrorem* as a warning to other criminals. This punishment was inflicted in the time of the Ikkeri Rájás, shortly before Haidar captured the town.

and feet of condemned men, and then to attach them by a rope to the foot of an elephant, which, being urged forwards, dragged them after it on the rough ground, and painfully terminated their existence. Some again were ruthlessly thrown into the dens of tigers to be devoured, and it is said that three of Tipú's high officials met with this fate. Cutting off of ears and noses was a general practice, and was frequently inflicted on defaulters, thieves, and peccant subordinates.

The personal appearance of Tipú Sultán is fairly well known from the many portraits of him which have been produced at various times, but he is generally represented as being fairer than he really was. In all the best likenesses one cannot fail to note a certain amount of complacent self-sufficiency, which was in fact the mainspring of his singularly eccentric character. He had small delicate hands and feet, showing his Indian descent by the mother's side, an aquiline nose, large lustrous eyes, the neck rather short and thick, and the body somewhat inclined to corpulency. He wore no beard, but, unlike his father, retained his eyebrows, eyelashes, and moustache. He is described as having been so modest that no one ever saw any part of his person, save his feet, ancles, and wrists; while in the bath he always covered himself from head to foot. The same delicacy of feeling induced him to prohibit women from going about with their head and bosom uncovered[1].

[1] This edict applied apparently to the western coast, where in

Unlike Haidar Alí, he ordinarily affected extreme simplicity of dress as more becoming to an orthodox believer, and enjoined the observance of the same rule on all his followers, but when proceeding on journeys he wore a coat of cloth of gold with a red tiger-streak embroidered on it. He generally wrapped a white handkerchief over his turban and under his chin. The turban in the later years of his life was of a green colour.

The popular error that Tipú is the Kanarese word for 'tiger' seems to have arisen in this way. The synonym for a lion (his father's name) would be in India 'a tiger,' lions being unknown in Southern India, and in order probably to strike terror into the minds of his subjects he adopted this ferocious beast as the emblem of his rule. It used to be said, that he declared he would sooner live two days as a tiger than two hundred years as a sheep. The uniform of his soldiers was embellished with a tiger-stripe, the same device being shown on his guns and other paraphernalia. According to the statements of his English prisoners, several live tigers were kept in cages or chained up in front of his palace.

On his weapons he had inscribed 'Asad Ullah al Ghálib,' that is 'the Lion of God (Alí, for whom he had a great reverence) is the conqueror.' The principal

former times women of the lower castes were forbidden to cover the upper part of the body in the presence of their superiors. It is related that the Queen of Attangadi ordered the breasts of a woman who had offended against this usage to be cut off.

ornament of his throne was a tiger's head of life-size, wrought in gold, which served as the support of the throne. The bas-reliefs of the throne, which was approached by silver steps, were decorated with tigers' heads worked in gold and adorned with precious stones. Over it was suspended a húmá, or bird of Paradise, whose brilliant wings, encrusted with diamonds, rubies, and emeralds, hovered over the Sultán[1]. The húmá formed the apex of a canopy, fringed with pearls, which was attached to a gilt pillar seven feet high.

After the first siege of Seringapatam Tipú always slept on coarse canvas instead of on a bed, and at his repasts listened to some religious book which was read out to him. Unlike his father Haidar, he never indulged in ribald conversation, but he was fond of enunciating his views on every possible subject, whether religion, morals, science, war, commerce, or any other topic of discourse. The words of wisdom which fell from his lips were received by his obsequious courtiers with all due humility and respect. Among the crowd

[1] At Windsor Castle are preserved the royal footstool of Tipú and the richly-jewelled bird which adorned the canopy of the throne. Among other relics of the Sultán are portions of his tent with silver poles, ivory chairs, elephant and horse trappings, a palankeen, two richly-ornamented field-pieces, and various weapons, including the sword and shield which were found with his body after the siege. In the library of the castle is a copy of the Korán, formerly belonging to the Emperor Aurangzeb, which was found among Tipú Sultán's treasures. It is said to have cost 9,000 rupees, and is beautifully written in the Naskh character, with elegant ornamentations.

of officials who surrounded him very few succeeded in retaining his confidence, and only one Hindu, the Bráhman Púrnaiya, was admitted to his inner counsels. This undoubtedly able man remained with him to the end. So did his finance minister, Mír Muhammad Sádik, a name held in execration by the peasantry on account of his rapacity and extortions. Tipú's most trusted commander was Búrhán-ud-dín, whose sister he had married, and to whom he confided the conduct of many military enterprises. Búrhán was killed in 1790 at Satyamangalam. A cousin, named Kamar-ud-dín Alí Khán, the son of Alí Razá, whose sister Haidar Alí had married, was sometimes placed at the head of a body of troops. But he was generally accompanied by more experienced generals, and never entirely trusted, while both he and Búrhán-ud-dín were encompassed by the Sultán's spies.

The distrust which he thus evinced towards his ablest servants, and especially during the latter part of his rule, seems to have been a radical defect in his character. It naturally led to his being taken in and deceived on all sides, his troops alone remaining faithful to him, notwithstanding the perpetual changes which he made in matters affecting their organization, discipline, and pay. From his youth upwards he was deficient in stability and straightforwardness, so much so as to excite the wrath of his father. Haidar, besides publicly flogging Tipú at Chinkuráli as has been previously mentioned, exacted from him an agreement, in which the youth declared that, if he commit theft or fraud, or be proved guilty of prevarication, misrepresentation, or deceit, or if he should be detected in taking presents without orders, or carrying on secret intrigues, he consents to be strangled, or to undergo some other condign punishment. It is evident from the contents of this curious paper, which was discovered at Seringapatam after the siege in 1799, that Haidar was well aware of the unstable and fickle temperament of his son. It was also asserted by many who knew Tipú in later life that his understanding was at times clouded over in a way that betrayed symptoms of mental aberration [1].

So many instances have been given of the atrocities which he committed in the name of religion, that it would be superfluous to add to them. In this respect he rivalled Mahmúd of Ghazní, Nádir Sháh, and Alá-ud-dín the Pathán Emperor of Delhi surnamed the Khúni, or the Bloody, all of whom were famous for the number of infidels slaughtered by their orders. For this very zeal for the faith, notwithstanding the cruelties which attended his persecutions, the name of Tipú Sultán was long held in reverence by his co-religionists in Southern India—a proof how readily

[1] Among the papers found in his library was a register of his dreams, some of which are not a little extraordinary. In one of these visions he saw a person dressed like a man, whom he caressed as if he were a woman, when the apparition suddenly threw off its garments, let down its hair, and exposed to view its bosom, which revealed a female form. Tipú deduced from this vision the fact that his enemies, the Maráthás, though clothed like men, were really only women in character.

crimes that cry to Heaven are condoned when the perpetrator of them is supposed to have been animated by a sincere desire to propagate the faith which he professed. On his tomb at Seringapatam, it is recorded, in phrases which, as in the case of Haidar Alí, commemorate by the *Abjad* system the year of his death, that the 'Haidarí Sultán' died for the faith. The words are 'Núr Islám wa dín z' dunyá raft,' i. e. 'The light of Islám and the faith left the world;' 'Tipú ba wajah dín Muhammad shahíd shud,' i. e. 'Tipú on account of the faith of Muhammad was a martyr;' 'Shamshér gúm shud,' i. e. 'The sword was lost;' 'Nasal Haidar shahíd akbar shud,' i. e. 'The offspring of Haidar was a great martyr,' all these phrases being supposed to represent the year 1213 Hijri, corresponding with A.D. 1799. The inscription was composed by Mír Hussén Alí, and was written by one Abd-ul-Kádir.

During the perilous days of the Mutiny, it is said that bigoted Musalmáns congregated at this spot to say their prayers and breathe secret aspirations for the re-ascendancy of their faith. As one stands in the tomb, words faintly uttered resound in hollow reverberations in the lofty dome, and one cannot help feeling a momentary compassion for a Sovereign who, tyrant and usurper as he was, died a soldier's death.

INDEX

ARCOT, Nawábs of, 21: their history, 21: pedigree of, 22: fort of, captured by Haidar, 93.

ÁRNI, action near, 103.

AURANGZEB, sends throne to Mysore Rájá, 15.

BADAR-UZ-ZAMÁN, defends Dhárwár, 159.

BAILLIE, Col., disastrous defeat of, at Perambákam, 91.

BAIRD, Gen., leads the assault at Seringapatam, 198: his humanity, 201.

BÁLÁJÍ RÁO PESHWÁ, invades Mysore, 28.

BANGALORE, captured by Lord Cornwallis, 152–154.

BÁRAMAHÁLS, ceded to Maráthás, 32: invaded by Haidar, 89.

BASÁLAT JÁNG, appoints Haidar Nawáb of Sírá, 34: cedes Guntúr to Madras Government, 81.

BEDARS, join Haidar, 25: capture Nijagal, 60: defend Chitaldrúg, 73–74.

BEDNÚR, early history of, 35: Sivappa Náyak of, 36: captured by Matthews, 120: recovered by Tipú, 122: fate of garrison, 123.

BELLARY, seized by Haidar, 68.

BOMBAY GOVERNMENT, the convention of Wargám, 81: sends troops to Malabar, 103: orders Gen. Matthews to seize Bednúr, 120.

CALICUT, seized by Haidar, 45.

CHÁMRÁJ RÁJÁ, death of, 68: strange selection of his successor, 68.

CHANDÁ SÁHIB, aided by the French, 23.

CHERKÚLI, action at, between Haidar and Maráthás, 61.

CHIKKA DEVARÁJ, his territory, 15.

CHIKKA KRISHNARÁJ RÁJÁ, death of, 47.

CHIRAKKAL, Rájá of, killed by Tipú, 137.

CHITALDRÚG, former history of, 72: attacked by Haidar, 73: captured by Haidar, 74.

COIMBATORE, invaded by Haidar, 56: its defence by Chalmers, 163.

COORG, Rájás of, 65: invaded by Haidar, 66: insurrection in, 68: Tipú's cruelty in the province of, 127: Rájá of, joins British, 169.

COOTE, Sir Eyre, assumes command in Madras, 93: relieves Wándiwásh, 94: action near Porto Novo, 95: and at Pollilúr, 96: encounters Haidar at Sholingarh, 97: throws supplies into Vellore, 98: encounters Haidar's troops near Árni, 103.

CORNWALLIS, Lord, declares war on Tipú, and makes an alliance with the Nizám and the Maráthás, 145: assumes command of the army, 151: besieges and captures Bangalore, 152–154: attacks Seringapatam, 156: compelled to retreat, 158: captures Nandidrúg, 163: assaults Sávandrúg, 165: besieges Seringapatam, 168: makes a treaty with Tipú, 171: his policy, 171.

DELLA VALLE, Italian traveller, 35.

DHÁRWÁR, captured by Haidar, 70: besieged by Parasu Rám Bháo, 159.

DUPLEIX, his masterly policy, 23.

FATAH MUHAMMAD, his descent, 12: his success, 13: his death, 17.

FAZL-ULLAH KHÁN, descends Gajalhátti Pass, 56.

FRENCH, artificers in Haidar's service, 27: gallant conduct under Lally, 99: their influence over Haidar, 106: their honourable conduct at Mangalore, 125: French Jacobins at Seringapatam, 175.

FULLARTON, Col., his expedition to Pálghát, 128: his march stopped by the Madras Government, 129.

GAJALHÁTTI PASS, descended by Haidar, 56: descended by Tipú, 147.

GÚTTI, surrendered to Haidar, 69.

HAIDAR ALÍ, his birth, 13: serves as a volunteer, 18: want of education, 18: seizes Nizám's treasure, 25: joins Muhammad Alí: employs Khande Ráo, 26: Fáujdár of Dindigal, 26: encounters Gopál Hari, 29: receives title from Mysore Rájá, 30: conspiracy against him, 31: is defeated, 32: appointed Dalwái, 33: overthrows Khande Ráo, 33: assumes the control of affairs, 33: appointed Nawáb of Sírá, 34: captures Bednúr, 38: seizes Sundá, 40: defeated by the Maráthás, 41: invades Malabar, 42: imprisons Samúri, 45: suppresses Náir insurrection, 45: attacked by Madhu Ráo, 47: attacks Col. Smith, 49: defeated near Trinomalai, 50: captures Mangalore, 51: seizes Múlbágal, 53: besieges Hosúr, 55: seizes Wood's guns, 55: enters Coimbatore, 56: defeats Capt. Nixon, 56: ready to make peace, but thwarted by Muhammad Alí, 57: his raid on Madras, 57: makes a treaty, 58: his defeat at Cherkúli, 61: sues for peace, 62: invades Coorg, 64: intrigues with Raghubá, 67: selects new Rájá, 68: captures Bellary, 68: seizes Gútti, 69: defeats Maráthás at Sáunsi, 70: attacks Chitaldrúg, 73: defeats Hari Panth, 74: captures Chitaldrúg, 74: his severe rule, 78: royal weddings, 78: his grievances against the English, 82: his straightforward conduct, 83: enters into correspondence with the French, 84: his reception of the Rev. Mr. Schwartz and Mr. Gray, 85: declares war on the English, 87: invades Madras territory, 88: defeats Col. Baillie, 90–92: reduces Arcot, 93: encounters Coote near Porto Novo, 95: fight at Pollidúr, 96: and near Sholingarh, 97: his conversation with Púrnaiya, 101: encounters Coote near Árni, 103: despatches Tipú to Malabar, 103: his death, 104: his character and administration, 106–113.

HARI PANTH, defeated by Haidar, 74.

HARRIS, Gen., assumes command, 190: defeats Tipú at Malvalli, 192: advances on Seringapatam, 193: prescribes terms of peace, 196: takes Seringapatam by assault, 198.

HASTINGS, Warren, his action on hearing of Baillie's defeat, 93: succeeds in detaching the Nizám and the Maráthás from Haidar, 100.

KADAPA NAWÁB, kills Násir Jang, 25: his territory seized by Haidar, 77.

KAMAR-UD-DÍN, captures Coimbatore, 164.

KHANDE RÁO enters Haidar's service, 26: his treachery, 31: his imprisonment, 34.

KOLÁR, birthplace of Haidar, 13.

MADHU RÁO PESHWÁ, invades Mysore, 40: defeats Haidar, 41: again invades Mysore, 47: last invasion by, 59.

MADRAS GOVERNMENT, takes steps to oppose Haidar, 52: makes a treaty with him, 58: its absurd confidence in Muhammad Alí, 58: its preparations to oppose Haidar's invasion, 89: apathy of, 119: arrests Fullarton's march on Malabar, 129: deprecates the hostile preparations of Lord Mornington, 182.

MAHÉ, captured by British troops, 84.

MALABAR, early history of, 42: mentioned by Camoens, 42–43: invaded by Haidar, 42: cruelty of Tipú in, 136.

MALVALLI, action at, 192.

MANGALORE seized by Haidar, 51: besieged and captured by Tipú, 124–125.

MARÁTHÁS invade Mysore, 28, 40, 47, 59: send an ambassador to Haidar, 80: abandon Haidar's cause, 100.

MAXWELL, Col., reconnoitres Krishnagiri, 148: attacked by Tipú, 149.

MEDOWS, Gen., his plan of campaign, 146: fails to force Gajalhátti Pass, 147.

MELUKOTE, shrine of, plundered by Maráthás, 62.

MORÁRI RÁO, joins Col. Smith, 52: surrenders Gútti to Haidar, 69.

MORNINGTON, Lord, negotiates with the Nizám and the Maráthás, 180–182: orders Madras Government to prepare for hostilities, 183: his statesman-like minute, 183: his correspondence with Tipú, 185: declares war, 189: appoints Gen. Harris to command the British army, 190: his judicious arrangements for disposing of Tipú's dominions, 203.

MUHAMMAD ALÍ, his evil influence with Madras Government, 57: sends an agent to England, 82: failure to aid the English, 88.

MÚLBÁGAL seized by Haidar, 53: action at, 54.

MUNRO, Sir H., his inaction at Conjevaram, 90.

MYSORE, ancient dynasties of, 13: pedigree of Rájás, 16.

NÁNÁ FARNAVÍS, opposes Raghubá, 67.

NANJRÁJ, minister, gives a command to Haidar, 18.

NANJRÁJ, Rájá, installed by Haidar, 47: strangled, 63.

NÁSIR JANG, seizes the throne, 23: killed by Kadapa Nawáb, 25.

NEGAPATAM, stormed by Col. Braithwaite, 99.

NIJAGAL, escalade of, 60.

NIZÁM, history of, 19 : pedigree of, 20.
NIZÁM ALÍ, joins the Maráthás, 49 : deserts the English, and joins Haidar, 49 : his grievances against the English, 81 : deserts Haidar, 100 : invests Kopal, 160 : his troops join Lord Cornwallis, 166 : disbands French contingent, 180 : sends troops to join Gen. Harris, 190.

PANNIÁNI, action at, 104.
PARASU RÁM BHÁO, besieges Dhárwár, 159.
PESHWÁS, pedigree of, 30.

RAGHUBÁ, intrigues with Haidar, 67.
RÁJ WODIAR, seizes Seringapatam, 15.

SALÁBAT JANG, invades Mysore, 28.
SAMÚRI OR ZAMORIN, early notice of, 42, 43 : submits to Haidar, 45 : his death, 45.
SÁVANÚR, Nawáb of, his matrimonial alliances with Haidar, 78 : town of, captured by Tipú, 133.
SCHWARTZ, his mission to Haidar, 85.
SERINGAPATAM, ancient history of, 167 : siege of, 168 : final siege of, 193–200 : present aspect of, 205.
SHÁHBÁZ, brother of Haidar Alí, receives a command, 18.
SHEKH AYÁZ, surrenders Bednúr to Matthews, 122.
SIDDHESHWAR, action at, 191.
SÍRÁ, headquarters of Imperial deputy, 17 : Haidar appointed Nawáb of, 34.
SMITH, Col., defeats Haidar near Trinomalai, 50 : acquires Krishnagiri, 52 : failure to draw Haidar into a general action, 55 : his recall, 55.
SUBLIME PORTE, its letter to Tipú, 186.
SULLIVAN, Mr., his plan for an expedition to Malabar, 128.

TIPÚ SULTÁN, present at defeat of Baillie, 91 : and at siege of Arcot, 93 : defeats Col. Braithwaite, 99 : attacks Panniáni, 104 : his birth, 117 : his accession, 118 : recaptures Bednúr, 122 : besieges Mangalore, 124 : his deportation of Malabar Christians, 125 : his edict on the subject, 126 : his cruelty in Coorg, 127 : detects a conspiracy at Seringapatam, 129 : treats the Madras envoys with contempt, 130 : his cruelty to his prisoners, 130 : attacks Nargúnd and Rámdrug, 131 : assumes title of King, 132 : attacks and razes Adoni, 132 : seizes Sávanúr, 133 : his reforms in Malabar, 135 : kills Rájá of Chirakkal, 137 : sends embassies to Europe, 137 : invades Travancore, 140 : his repulse and subsequent victory, 141–143 : descends Gajalhátti Pass, 147 : attacks Gen. Medows, 147 : and Col. Maxwell, 149 : escapes by Thopúr Pass, 149 : ravages the Coromandel, 150 : his troops defeated in Malabar, 151 : tries to stop Lord Cornwallis' advance on Bangalore, 151 : his conduct at the siege, 153–155 : murders Europeans at Seringapatam, 155 : defends his capital, 156 : submits to Lord Cornwallis' terms, 171 : bombastic effusions, 172 : intrigues with Alí Jáh, 174 : and with Zamán Sháh, 175 : sends an embassy to Mauritius, 177 : his correspondence with Lord Mornington, 185 : his evasive letter, 188 : attacks Bombay force at Siddheshwar, 191 : encounters Gen. Harris at Malvalli, 192 : prepares to defend

Seringapatam, 193: sends an agent to Gen. Harris' camp, 195: refuses terms proffered, 197: prepares to fight to the last, 197: is wounded, and killed by an English soldier, 199: search for his body, 200: his funeral, 200: his character and administration, 208–227.

TRAVANCORE, the lines of, 139: invaded by Tipú, 140–144.

TRIMBAK RÁO, defeats Haidar at Cherkúli, 61.

VELLORE, besieged by Haidar, 97; garrison relieved by Coote, 98.

WÁNDIWÁSH, gallantly defended by Lieut. Flint, 89, 94.

WELLESLEY, Col., his repulse at Sultánpet Tope, 194.

WOOD, Col., joins Col. Smith, 50: fights at Trinomalai: attacked by Haidar at Múlbágal, 54: loses all his guns, 55: recalled, 56.

THE END.